D1519670

Writing on the Internet
Finding a Voice Online

Marcia Peoples Halio
University of Delaware

Harcourt Brace College Publishers

Fort Worth   Philadelphia   San Diego   New York   Orlando   Austin   San Antonio
Toronto   Montreal   London   Sydney   Tokyo

To
Ben, Eric, Connor, and
Brendan
Writers of the Future

Publisher:	Earl McPeek
Acquisitions Editor:	Michael Rosenberg/Julie McBurney
Product Manager:	Laura Brennan
Developmental Editor:	Diane Drexler
Project Editor:	Matt Ball/Michele Tomiak
Art Director:	Candice Johnson Clifford
Production Manager:	Kathleen Ferguson

ISBN: 0-15-505503-8

Library of Congress Catalog Card Number: 97-80909

Address for orders:
Harcourt Brace College Publishers
6277 Sea Harbor Drive
Orlando, FL 32887-6777
1-800-782-4479

Address for editorial correspondence:
Harcourt Brace College Publishers
301 Commerce Street, Suite 3700
Fort Worth, TX 76102

Web site address:
http://www.hbcollege.com

Printed in the United States of America

9 0 1 2 3 4 5 6 7 039 9 8 7 6 5 4 3 2

ACKNOWLEDGMENTS

No textbook comes into being without the help and support of many people.

Special thanks to the students whose writing appears in this book: Nancy Matthews, David Persoleo, Allyson B., Harlan Landes, Bryan Jariwala, Andrea Schenk, Heather D'Agostino, Kyle Belz, Ashley Booth, Sue Dumbauld, Sarah Wilson, Mary Heim, Holly Donofrio, Kristy Redford, Rich Cook, Tony Barbone, and Jennifer McKinley. Because of their contributions, this book has many strong voices.

Thanks also to the instructors and graduate teaching assistants in the Writing Program at the University of Delaware who provided ideas and support and tested many of the exercises. Daily, they show me new ways to teach writing with technology.

The reviewers—John Clark, Bowling Green State University; William Condon, Washington State University; Mary Lou Crouch, George Mason University; Marla Dinchak, Glendale Community College; and Michael Palmquist, Colorado State University—helped me to focus my thoughts. Many times, their enthusiasm for the project sustained me when my energy was flagging.

Finally, I would like to thank Diane Drexler, developmental editor at Harcourt Brace, who gave me excellent advice every step of the way, and Michael Rosenberg, executive editor, who believed in this project from the start.

Chapter Five introduces students to the most exciting part of Internet writing: creating a World Wide Web page. In this chapter, students learn the basics of HTML (Hypertext Markup Language), the simple computer language used to create pages. They also learn how to critique Web pages and then build a simple page of their own. After building a personal page, students visit online research papers written by students at other colleges or universities. They analyze them, looking for the difficulties created by the new ways of writing demanded by reading on the screen. Finally, students build a hypertextual argument, converting a linear essay into a Web document and publishing it to the world. They also debate issues of copyright and censorship.

In the appendices, students can find a reference for documenting online sources in MLA format, a reference for using Pine e-mail, advanced HTML tags for Web pages, and suggestions for participating in real-time discussions using MUD (Multi-User Dimension) and MOO (MUD Object Oriented) technology.

Throughout this book, technical discussion is kept to a minimum. Although different schools may be using different hardware and software to access the Internet, the concepts are generalizable. If one learns to use one e-mail package, one can use another. If one learns to use one WWW browser, one can use another. You may wish to supplement this text with handouts on e-mail, Listservs, Web browsers, and HTML publishing from the computer labs on your campus. You may also find that some of the students in your classroom are expert users of the technology. They may not be excellent writers, but they can become technology helpers to other students and even to you, increasing their self-esteem.

Students who complete the material in this book will have a great deal of practice writing and learning about this new medium. They will be better prepared as writers to enter the twenty-first century.

Are you a motivated writer? If not, perhaps it's because you have always felt that you were writing for no other purpose than to achieve a desired grade. Your writing had no real meaning for you nor any life after the course was over.

The teacher may have asked you to imagine that you were writing for a particular audience or purpose, but in reality, you knew that was just a game. For you, the audience was the person who would give you the grade, and the purpose was to get the highest grade possible.

Writing on the Internet changes the rules of that game. When you write online, you have access to real audiences and real purposes. Via e-mail, you can contact classmates on your own campus and engage in discussions about class assignments, readings in the text, or the meaning of life. Because e-mail is somewhere between a phone call and a letter, you have time to think about the message you are creating, yet you can retain the informal, conversational style of a phone call.

Using Listservs, you can subscribe to a mailing list where people of similar interests debate issues, provide information, and help one another to solve problems. You can find a new community. You can also participate in Usenet groups, the ham radio of the Internet. Usenet groups range from friendly and informal to serious and professional. They also contain the most vitriolic hate mail and the most offensive material on the Net. When people talk about censoring the Internet, they are usually talking about Usenet groups. If you join a discussion, you will confront real people about real issues. They may not necessarily be polite or courteous, but they will challenge you to use your words to express yourself clearly and forcefully. You may discover a voice you didn't know you had and a satisfaction in using writing to defend a point of view.

You can also use the research possibilities of the Internet, including the World Wide Web, to provide your voice with an authority that it may have lacked in the past. Daily, millions of pieces of information are posted on the Net, much of it in home pages on the Web. You can use search engines to quickly find information to defend your point of view or to understand the viewpoints of others.

Finally, you can learn how to publish your work to the world by using a computer language (HTML) to add tags or codes to your documents and posting them to a home page you create on the Web. Once you post your work, you can be certain that it will have a life after the course is over. You can connect your page to other sites on the Web with links and update your page when you have some new ideas. You can use your home page to reach a potential audience of millions.

When you have practiced writing on the Internet, you can experience the publishing possibilities for the twenty-first century. You will be part of the revolution that is transforming the way people read, write, and think. Your writing will have power impossible in the past. You will be entering a truly democratic forum for discussion where the quality of your words can introduce you to communities you may never have had a chance to experience before.

Enjoy *Writing on the Internet!*

CONTENTS

C H A P T E R

O N E

E-MAIL: SENDING A LETTER TO THE WORLD

"Changing Human Relationships in Cyberspace"
By Ashley Booth

I love e-mail! I am on the computer two or three times a day checking to see if someone has decided to write to me. My experiences with this way of communicating have been very positive. I e-mail my Dad once a day telling him what I am doing. This is a great alternative to talking on the phone every night: e-mail saves me from making my phone bill skyrocket! Through e-mail, our relationship has also gotten better. I can talk to him whenever I want to, and I don't have to wait for him to finish something so that he can talk to me. When he writes me back, I have the option of whether or not to respond to a comment he made. Due to this, there is no confrontation, so I don't have come up with a response that might hurt one of us: I can think about what I want say. I also "talk" to my cousin online a couple of times a week. We see each other only once a year, and talking with her this way has brought us much closer than before. She knows all the details of my life, and I know all of hers. Before college, we never talked to each other except on birthdays. Now I wouldn't give up my chance to talk with her every day for anything in the world!

GETTING ACQUAINTED WITH E-MAIL

E-mail is a new type of communication: a cross between a phone call and a letter, electronic mail has some of the characteristics of both. Like a phone call, it is often spontaneous, friendly, and informal; however, unlike a phone call, it can wait a while before the reader answers a writer's question or supplies information. On the phone, if the boss asks for the data for a project, or a friend asks for an opinion on some important topic, it's hard to wait and take the time to think of a good response. But with e-mail, you can often postpone an answer until you have had a chance to think about the message you received.

Like a letter, e-mail bears your "signature," either in a custom file you create or just in the heading at the top of the message; and it can become a permanent record, stored in a file online or in hard copy. However, because e-mail *seems* so informal and friendly, writers often do not carefully check punctuation, grammar, content, and tone of voice before sending a message. They also do not always consider the reactions of the person who will receive the message. Ordinarily, important letters sit on desks overnight, or for a few hours, before they are signed and sealed into an envelope. But e-mail can be sent across campus or across the globe with a few keystrokes. Somehow the phosphorous glowing on the screen prompts writers to act too quickly. *It's important to remember that readers can form a long-lasting impression of you from a hastily sent message.*

So, watch out: to learn to use e-mail effectively, do the exercises in this chapter. Practice writing to various audiences for various purposes until you become comfortable with this new way to make your voice heard effectively by readers around the campus or around the world.

GETTING CONNECTED TO E-MAIL

To use e-mail, you must be writing on a computer attached to a network. Perhaps you are using a modem and an account with a commercial bulletin board service on an IBM type of computer running Microsoft Windows; or you may be using a Macintosh with a direct Ethernet connection to a network. In either case, you must learn how to access the Internet from your system. After you have accessed the Net, you can log on to your system and load the software for e-mail. To learn how to access the system and log on, you will probably need to check with your instructor or with the campus computing services. Following is some basic information you will need to know.

First, check to see how you connect to the mail server. If you are working at a remote location without direct connection to the mail server (for example, in a residence hall or at home), you will need *communications software.* You will also need a *network card in your computer.*

HARDWIRED?

Some residence halls are "hardwired" to the mail server; that is, they have a direct connection. Check to see if that is the case for your residence hall. If so, you will not need communications software, but you will still need the network (probably Ethernet) card for the inside of your central processing unit (CPU).

Once you have established connections to the mail server, you are ready to log on and load the software to do e-mail.

You can usually obtain handouts on using your mail system from campus computing support services. Find this service and contact it for documentation, or instructions, regarding logging on to e-mail. Probably, workers there will issue you a *user ID,* which you can change to a word (often your last name and an initial) after you log on for the first time. You will also be asked to choose a *password* to protect the privacy of your files. Remember that e-mail is never really private. Archives are kept and system operators often have access to the archives. *Do not put anything of a very private or sensitive nature in e-mail.*

Changing a User ID   Some systems allow you to change your user ID. Check to see if this is possible at your school.

If so, you might want to change your number identification to a *word.* It's usually best to choose your last name and one of your initials. For example, if you are Emily Dickinson, you might choose a user name such as *EDickinson.* If you want to establish a wide base of e-mail correspondents, it's important to choose an ID that will be easy for correspondents to remember or to locate. Also, cute or idiosyncratic user IDs such as *snowwhite* or *robinhood* might be fun for a while, but they quickly lose their charm when you are applying for a job or corresponding for professional or business purposes. To change the user ID issued by your campus computing office to your name, you must first log on using the ID issued to you. Then, following the handouts issued by the office, type the command to change your ID.

Choosing a Password   Choose a password that will not be easy for a "hacker" to guess. Usually a good password is made up of a combination of numbers and letters or characters that do not make sense. For example, if I used my initials and my phone number as my password (*ed2297*), it would be fairly easy for a hacker to break my security. But if I used some combination of seemingly unrelated numbers and characters and letters such as *poems24,* it would be much harder for my security to be breached. So, be safe: create a secure password and change it from time to time. *Do not tell your password to anyone. Choose a password you can remember.*

Once you have an account on a mail server connected to the Internet, a user ID, a password, and access to the software to run a mail program such as Pine, Netscape Navigator, Microsoft Explorer, Elm, or Eudora, you are ready to write e-mail. To use e-mail efficiently, you need to know how to compose a message, reply to a message, save messages in folders, delete messages, forward messages, and create an address book for frequent correspondents. All of these are easy to do using the standard e-mail software. In this chapter you will practice writing messages and responses, saving messages and using them in your essays, and forwarding messages effectively. *For information on how to use your software to do these tasks, refer to your documentation or the handouts from your campus computing services.* Handouts created by computing services are usually much easier to understand than the documentation that comes with the software. In general, e-mail software usually needs no more than two or three pages of documentation if it is clearly written (see the Appendix C for a sample of Pine e-mail instructions).

E-Mail Addresses   E-mail addresses consist of two parts, with an @ sign (spoken as "at") separating the "username" (the user ID) from the "domain name," the name of the location of the "host" computer for the person you are writing to. For example, my e-mail address is *EDickinson@xyzu.edu.* My username is *EDickinson,* and *xyzu.edu* is the name of the host computer. Conveniently, all computers at educational institutions have a domain name that ends in *.edu.* Other common endings are *.gov* (government), *.org* (organization such as Greenpeace), *.mil* (military), and *.com* (commercial or business). Domain names can also end with abbreviations for foreign countries, such as *.it* (Italy) or *.fr* (France). *The most reliable way to obtain addresses is to ask the addressee.* Or, you can consult online directories by using Gopher searches or the World Wide Web (Web or WWW). See the end of this chapter for an example of ways to search the Web for addresses. Consult your teacher or your lab director for ways to use Gopher to find e-mail addresses.

UPPER- OR LOWERCASE LETTERS?

Many computer systems are "case sensitive": that is, they recognize uppercase and lowercase letters as entirely different characters; therefore, it is important to use the correct form. Most e-mail addresses are lowercase.

Finding E-Mail Addresses   You can learn how to find e-mail addresses by using the resources of the Internet such as Gopher or Lynx or one of the search engines on the World Wide Web to visit the home pages of a school, organization, or business. For tips on locating e-mail addresses, see the sample search of WWW sites at the end of this chapter. Also see Chapter 4 for practice finding addresses using search tools.

PRACTICE SENDING MESSAGES

:-> :-) **Try This** :-O ;-)

Send a Practice Message to Yourself Now that you have logged on to the system and loaded the e-mail software (Pine, Elm, Eudora, and so forth) try sending a message to yourself. At the address prompt, enter your user ID and the rest of your address. Press Enter to move on to the next prompt.

If your mail program gives you a place for a carbon copy (CC), try typing your ID and domain name in that space. If this works, you should receive *two* copies of your message.

At the prompt for the subject, type a word or phrase that clearly indicates the content of your message. Since e-mail messages are listed in the recipient's mailbox by the name of the sender and the subject line, you should get into the habit of being precise with subject lines. Often, recipients may delete or skip over a mail message that has only a generic subject line such as "essay" or "assignment." And, by all means, *never leave the subject line blank:* some mail systems automatically delete messages with no subject.

Write a subject line that will tell potential readers clearly what your message is about. For example, if you are writing a message about the first assignment, which is to mail a message to yourself, you might use a subject line that reads *mail to self.*

When you have entered the address, the carbon copy, and the subject line, move the cursor down to the message area and type a message to yourself. Be playful here. Often writers become tense when using a new technology. *The secret to finding a voice online is to be yourself.* Talk to yourself in your normal tone of voice. Imagine that you are telling yourself to "Get with it" or "Stop procrastinating." Talk to yourself out loud, online.

Now send the message to yourself. When it pops into your Inbox, retrieve it and read it. Do you sound natural? If not, try again.

:-> :-) **Try This** :-O ;-)

Send a Message to Classmates Now that you have sent a message to yourself, try reaching out to others. If you are working in a lab with other students, swap addresses and write to each other. Or if you are working alone, look in your school's phone book or online in the Gopher (see instructions, Chapter 4) for e-mail addresses of other students on campus. Write a message with a clear sense of audience and purpose. For example, you might introduce yourself to one of your classmates by writing a message about your hobbies and interests or your classes or major. Remember that few people carefully read messages longer than one screenful, so be concise. Ask yourself what parts of your life might be most interesting to your classmates. You might want to play with several versions of your message before sending it out.

If your class is on a *listserv* (see Chapter 2), try sending your mail message to the whole list, indicating your subject matter clearly in the subject line. In this case, if you are interested, for example, in astronomy or cooking, other students with similar interests may read your message and reply. You will start building a community.

:-> :-) Try This :-O ;-)

Writing Introductions   With any kind of writing, but especially with introductions, it is important to be aware of your *subject, audience,* and *purpose.* To see how students responded to my invitation to introduce themselves to their classmates, read the messages below. Which introductions do you find most effective? Why? Write a response to two or three messages and send it to the writer.

ON TUE, 10 SEP 1996, EDICKINSON WROTE TO HER E110.106 CLASS:

> Hi.
> Welcome to English online.
>
> Please press R (or CMD R if you're on a Mac)and write a message
> introducing yourself to the class. Talk about your interests, your
> major, whatever you wish.
>
> Then, write a new subject line: Move the arrow to end of the
> subject line. Use the Backspace key to erase the message that's
> there. Add one of your own that will get readers' attention.
>
> EDickinson   EDickinson@strauss.xyzu.edu
> English Department
>

ASHLEY'S RESPONSE:

Date: Tue, 10 Sep 1996 15:02:51 -0400 (EDT)

From: Ashley Marie Booth <00725@xyzu.edu>

To: EDickinson <EDickinson@xyzu.edu>

Cc: engl110-106@xyzu.edu

Subject: Re: Hello. Anybody there?

Hi, everybody! I'm Ashley. I'm going to do this quickly, because I've been typing for an hour!! This e-mail stuff is addictive! Have fun "surfing the Web", and if you want to write to me my number is 00725. See you in class on Thursday!

BRYAN'S RESPONSE:

Date: Tue, 10 Sep 1996 15:21:32 -0400 (EDT)

From: Lakshman <lakshman@xyzu.edu>

To: EDickinson <EDickinson@xyzu.edu>

Cc: engl110-106@xyzu.edu

Subject: Re: Hello. Anybody there?

Hey,
My name is Bryan Jariwala, and I am in English 110. Just saying hi to everyone. If you are bored drop me a couple of lines or something.
Bryan

SUE'S RESPONSE:

Hello E110!
My name is Sue Dumbauld, and I am a sophomore here at Delaware. I am from Hershey, PA. Last year I was a business major (too many math courses for me!), but I decided to switch into the Communications Department. Hopefully I will get a job in public relations and advertising someday. I like exercising and watching sports, especially college basketball. That's about it from me, I hope to get to know everyone throughout the semester!! Good Luck!!!
—Sue Dumbauld

ANDREA'S RESPONSE:

From: Andrea Faith Schenk <aschenk@xyzu.edu>

To: EDickinson <EDickinson@xyzu.edu>

Cc: engl110-106@xyzu.edu

Subject: All about Andrea

Hi! I'm in the 9:30 English 110 class, you know one of the three who showed up a half hour late on the first day of class! My name is Andrea Schenk and I'm living in Rodney. I'm from Essex County New Jersey and I'm majoring in Communication. I'm just learning how to do this e-mail thing, It's turning out to be a lot of fun! Much more economical than calling all my other friends at different schools! Well, I guess I'll see you all on Thurs.

SARAH'S RESPONSE:

Date: Wed, 11 Sep 1996 17:05:05 -0400 (EDT)

From: Sarah Margar Wilson <07883@xyzu.edu>

To: EDickinson <EDickinson@xyzu.edu>

Subject: Re: Hello. Anybody there?

> Hello, my name is Sarah and I just opened my EMail account today. My major is Communication and I am really excited about being a member in the freshmen class. Right now I have 11 other messages to reply to so I will write again soon.

MARY'S RESPONSE:

Date: Wed, 11 Sep 1996 18:55:36 -0600

From: 03120@xyzu.edu

To: EDickinson <EDickinson@xyzu.edu>

Subject: Re: Hello. Anybody there?

> Hi! My name is Mary Heim. I am also in English 110 in the Science lab. I have no idea how to do e-mail, so I hope this gets to someone! I am from Moorestown, New Jersey. I don't really understand the homework that's due tomorrow, so if anyone does, please help!!!

DAVID'S RESPONSE:

Date: Thu, 12 Sep 1996 18:02:49 -0400 (EDT)

From: David Mich Persoleo <dpersoleo@xyzu.edu>

To: Andrea Faith Schenk <aschenk@xyzu.edu>

Cc: EDickinson <EDickinson@xyzu.edu>, engl110-106@xyzu.edu

Subject: Re: All about Andrea

> Hey what's up? My name is David Persoleo. I live in Rodney D and don't like sending e-mail because it takes too long. But English class is fun and interesting. Anyway I'll see you in class.

HOLLY'S RESPONSE:

Date: Thu, 12 Sep 1996 20:56:54 -0400 (EDT)

From: Holly Ann Donofrio <01959@xyzu.edu>

To: David Mich Persoleo <dpersoleo@xyzu.edu>

Cc: Andrea Faith Schenk <aschenk@xyzu.edu>,
        EDickinson <EDickinson@xyzu.edu>, engl110-106@xyzu.edu

Subject: Re: All about Andrea

Hi! My name is Holly Donofrio. I'm in your English class. I just
wanted to say hi. This email stuff is pretty cool. Well I gotta go. I
have work to do.

COPY AND PASTE TO E-MAIL

You can compose in your word-processing program and cut and
paste the message to mail if you have software that will permit this,
such as Windows 95 or Mac System 7.
Ask your instructor for directions.

Try This

Send a Message to Students at Other Schools   Using the principles of e-mail
discussed above, send a message on some topic to a friend at another campus.
If you know the address of a friend at another school, or if you think you can
guess the address (for example, *gjones@penn.edu*), try writing a message now.
You can find e-mail addresses in online directories using Gopher and the
WWW. See Chapter 4 for instructions on using Gopher, or ask your instructor.
      Include a specific subject line and think carefully about how to arrange
your message. *Remember that e-mail is different from paper mail.* If you
write a long, newsy message, the recipient may read carefully only the first

"BOUNCED" MESSAGES

After you send your message, check your Inbox to see if it "bounces"
back to you. If you have made a mistake in the address, the post-
master or gatekeeper will send your mail back with some sort of
"error message" attached. *Since systems don't always work perfectly,
you will probably get error messages from time to time.* Sometimes
the problem is with you; sometimes it is with the computer on your
campus or on the receiving end. If your message bounces, check the
address carefully and try again.

screenful and press R to respond. Usually, it's a good idea to use the first sentence or paragraph to summarize your message and to give readers a hint of what's in the main message. That way, they will be able to choose which parts to read carefully and which to skim.

:-> :-) Try This :-O ;-)

Send a Message to Teachers   E-mail is a great way to stay in touch with teachers. If you don't understand an assignment, or if you must be absent from class, just drop the teacher a line. Remember, though, that you are writing to a teacher, not a friend. Before writing, think about the kind of relationship you have with this teacher in the classroom. Are you on a first-name basis in class? If so, chances are first names will work in e-mail. If not, maintain a more formal tone. Also, *be as specific as possible about your confusion with the assignment*. Don't just say, "I don't understand the assignment"; rather, say exactly *what* you don't understand. That way, the teacher will be able to give you a better answer. Many teachers give out their e-mail address the first day of class. If your teacher did not give out his or her address, it is probably available in a campus phone book—online or offline—or from the department office.

Sample Messages to a Teacher   Sue needed clarification of an assignment. Note that she wrote her message at 10:39 PM, and I answered it soon after that. Sometimes, e-mail gives students instant feedback. Of course, you shouldn't expect your teacher to be online 24 hours a day.

Date: Tue, 10 Sep 1996 20:39:36 -0400 (EDT)

From: Susan Kate Dumbauld <susied@xyzu.edu>

To: EDickinson <EDickinson@xyzu.edu>

Subject: Thursday's Assignment

Ms. Dickinson,
I don't quite understand the assignment for Thursday. I know we have to read the introduction of [the textbook] and write a one page paper on it. I just don't know what the paper's focus should be. I would really appreciate it if you could write back.
Thanks a lot!!
—Sue Dumbauld

The following week, Kristy Redford needed some help:

Date: Mon, 16 Sep 1996 15:36:21 -0400 (EDT)

From: Kristy Lynn Redford <06158@xyzu.edu>

To: EDickinson <EDickinson@xyzu.edu>

Subject: Eng110

Hi! I finally activated my e-mail account and wanted to try it out. But I also have a question regarding the one-page statement we are supposed to write for homework. I am not sure if I am interpreting the topic correctly. Am I really just answering the question: What would life be like if I were illiterate? I would appreciate any help you could give me.

Thanks, Kristy Redford

When Kristy discovered that she could get useful information using e-mail, she made use of this form of communication often during the semester, and her writing became more focused and more powerful.

ON SEPT. 19 (A SUNDAY), KRISTY WROTE:

Hi Ms. Dickinson! Sorry to disturb you on a weekend, but I am having some trouble with my essay. I am still torn between several different topics. One topic I would really like to try is how literacy has affected the life of someone I know. She is a patient with M.S. and can only communicate through use of a special electronic device on her computer. Yet she is also a writer. Is this topic okay to continue with? (also should the paper be double-spaced?) Any help would be appreciated.

Thanks,

  Kristy Redford

I was really delighted that Kristy wrote to me. Although the general theme of the course was *literacy,* I was eager for students to find their own "angle" on the topic—an angle that would interest them and motivate them to find a voice. Kristy's essay about her friend's use of writing to cope with health problems was so powerful I asked her if I could submit it to a first-year writing contest. If Kristy had not written e-mail, she might not have taken a chance to "own" her essay and write about a subject terribly important to her. Instead, she might have stuck to writing about literacy as it had been defined by her fellow students.

Another student, Ashley, was in a quandary on Sunday evening at 11:00 about the difference between "showing" and "telling," so she wrote the following message:

E110.106 Date: Sun, 22 Sep 1996 20:56:52 -0400 (EDT)

    From: Ashley Marie Booth <00725@xyzu.edu>

      To: EDickinson@xyzu.edu

    Subject: question about essay#1

> Hi, Ms. Dickinson! I have a question about the essay questions.
> What do you mean when you say "show, DON'T tell"? Thanks!!
> Ashley Booth

Sensing that Ashley might not be the only confused student, I forwarded my answer to the whole class list. Many students must have read that message, because the papers were much stronger at depicting powerful scenes in a narrative when they were submitted the following Tuesday.

:-> :-) Try This :-O ;-)

Send a Message to Nonacademics   If you want to write to a government agency to get information, for example, on current legislation on environmental protection, you can get e-mail addresses from government documents in the library, or online from the Web or Gopher or Lynx. But often, you can guess at addresses for the government or for businesses. For example, the e-mail address for letters to the editor at the *New York Times* is editor@ nytimes.com. For the White House, the address is president@whitehouse .gov. Try your luck. If the message bounces back to you, try again. Remember, though, that you are writing formal business correspondence. As one of my students said recently when she was writing to the vice president, "You have to sound intelligent!"

To sound professional and scholarly, ask for specific information. Don't just ask for the latest news about the environment. Instead, ask for information regarding pending legislation on the protection of a particular treasure such as the Chesapeake Bay or the redwood forests. A common suffix for environmental or charitable organizations such as Greenpeace is *.org.* You can often locate the e-mail address by typing *postmaster@nameoforg.org.* If you want to write e-mail to find out about the problems of homeless people in your community, you might try writing to *city* (substitute the name of your city) *.gov.*

For example, if you write to your city government about solutions for homeless people, you might write a message similar to this one:

To: mayor@chicago.gov

> Dear Sir:
> Recently, on my way to the university, I noticed several homeless people living under the bridge at 54th Street. I think the city needs to do something to provide shelter for them since the forecast is for well below freezing. Where will these people be able to spend the night? And what is the city doing about a long-term solution to this problem?

This message is specific and to the point. It would probably get an answer. It might even get some help for the people under the bridge!

Write an e-mail message to someone in government or business. Ask for specific information for a project you are working on in this class or in some other class. Be specific and to the point. Share the results of your message with your classmates online or face-to-face.

:-> :-) **Try This** :-O ;-)

Send a Message to International Readers Writing a message to international readers requires tact and finesse. Often international readers have different expectations about formality and tone than Americans. They may also be extremely sensitive to language issues. Americans expect everyone to read and write English fluently. Of course, many people in other lands do, but sometimes they do not. It is important to convey a sense of respect for language and culture when writing to international readers. It is also important to remember that Internet access is very uneven across the world. In some countries such as the United States, millions of people are online; however, in third-world countries, very few writers have access to the Net. Although the Internet looks like a democratic forum, not everyone is equally represented. To communicate effectively, you should be aware of the unequal distribution of power online. Keep in mind that the people you are communicating with have the power of online access. They may not be typical of people in the larger community in their country.

BE SAFE AND SURE

f your response is confidential or sensitive, the safest way to be sure that your response goes *only to the individual* and not to the whole group is to type the *individual's* address at the To: prompt.

Try writing a message to a reader from another culture and language background. What kinds of information would the reader expect? What kinds of sensitivities should you show regarding language?

If you need an e-mail address for an international reader, try writing to penpals@snark.ukma.kiev.va or echalk@cleo.murdoch.edu.au.

Note: Addresses for foreign students change frequently. The best way to locate international students to chat with is to check the Web. If you use a search engine such as AltaVista and type *students and email,* you will get the URLs for several sites where you can find e-mail addresses.

PRACTICE REPLYING TO A MESSAGE

:-> :-) **Try This** :-O ;-)

Reply to a Message   When you reply to a message, there are some basic conventions to follow. First, look carefully at the header in the message sent to you. Sometimes the mail is from one individual to you alone. Other times it is a mass mailing. Check to see if the message is from a list or from an individual. If you wish to respond only to the individual who wrote the message and not to the group, you should choose to reply just to the writer. In a listserv message, the Reply to: address usually indicates the name of a group or organization rather than an individual. For example: From: Jane Smith<js@unev.edu> Reply to: Wricam@mailbase.ac.uk. *If your response is confidential or sensitive, the safest way to be sure that your response goes only to the individual and not to the whole group is to type the individual's address at the* To: *prompt.* Then, think about the response you want to send. Usually, if you press R, or CMD R,to respond, the software will ask if you want to include the original message. In order not to clutter up the response, include the message, but edit it down, deleting the lines, sentences, or paragraphs that do not need to be included. Often it is important to include at least a sentence or two from the original note to remind the sender of his or her original message.

   Practice writing a response to one of the messages in your Inbox. After you have pressed the command key to respond, answer the questions asked by the software about replying to the individual or to the group. Then move your cursor to the lines that are unnecessary and delete them. (In Pine, use Control K to delete lines.) Next, move the cursor to places in the message where you want to answer questions or make comments. Check your software to see how to move up and down a screen (In Pine, Control Y and Control V). When you have finished writing interlinearly (between the lines), you may want to add a brief greeting or introduction.

   Note: You can compose in your word processor and cut and paste the message to mail if you have software that will permit this, such as Windows 95 or Mac System 7.

:-> :-) **Try This** :-O ;-)

Match the Tone: Formality vs. Informality   Some e-mail writers are very businesslike. Their messages are brief and to the point. They may say things such as

The Committee will meet at 2 pm on Wednesday to discuss the evaluation of new courses.

Of course, if you reply to such a message, you will probably want to be just as brief. Perhaps you will ask *where* the meeting will be!

But if you receive a message that opens with "Hello, good to see you on-line!" you will probably want to write a chatty, conversational note. Practice matching your tone to the tone of the sender. Look for clues such as sentence length, word complexity, and the presence or absence of "emoticons," cute pictures such as 8-) (see pp. 30–31). Try adjusting your voice to the formality or informality of the sender.

To practice matching the tone of your recipient, open one of your e-mail messages and analyze the level of formality or informality. Then respond to the message, trying to match the writer's tone.

Avoid "Flames"   Because e-mail is a "hot" medium—that is, messages are often written and responded to in haste, sometimes discussions can get very heated. If someone sends you a message that seems insulting, resist the impulse to answer it immediately. Instead, read it again and postpone replying. *Also, resist the impulse to attack anyone else online.* Sometimes it feels safe and comfortable to hide behind the screen and keyboard and say things you would never say in person, or even on the phone. But once an insult or a derogatory comment is sent, it's impossible to get it back. What's more, messages are stored in distant archives. Old, hastily sent messages can arise to haunt you.

BUILD AN ADDRESS BOOK

:-> :-) **Try This** :-O ;-)

Build an Address Book   Most mail systems allow you to keep an "address book" of frequent correspondents. Check to see how to do this with your software (see the Appendix for instructions for Pine). If you have an address book, it will be easy for you to create nicknames for your correspondents. This way, you will not have to type their whole address each time you want to write to them: instead, you just type the nickname, and the software will fill in the rest of the address. Also, if you have an address book, you can create mailing lists of your own. For example, if you are working on a collaborative project with other students in your class, you can use your address book to create a list of the members of the group. That way, you can easily keep in touch with each other about the progress of your project simply by writing to the list. You will need to meet face-to-face (ftf, in e-mail shorthand) less often, keeping the frustration of finding a time that everyone can get together to a minimum.

Practice saving at least three e-mail addresses in your address book. If you need help with the software, ask the teacher or a site assistant.

KEEP AN ONLINE JOURNAL

:-> :-) **Try This** :-O ;-)

Keep an Online Journal   Many writers like to keep an online journal of messages to themselves. You can drop yourself a line regularly, or whenever an idea strikes. It is easy to store these messages in file folders and use them in projects or to forward to others when they are ready for public viewing. Try keeping an online journal for a month or so. See if it is helpful to you. Such journals are often especially helpful when you are beginning to organize major projects such as research papers. You can store your own ideas and brainstorms, or you can cut and paste information from online library catalogs, databases, or the World Wide Web into your journal. Share the results of your online journal with your classmates, either online or face-to-face.

USE E-MAIL TO BUILD A RESOURCE FILE

:-> :-) **Try This** :-O ;-)

Use E-mail to Build a Resource File   When you receive interesting messages, save them in files to be used later. For example, if you are writing a research paper on censorship of the Internet, send a survey to classmates or distant correspondents and store the responses in a file called *Survey. Get writers' permission to use the comments in your paper.*

When you do some library research or research on the WWW, you can compare the results of your own survey to the information in the scholarly sources and you can write about this comparison in your paper. Resource files are very handy. Try using some to give your writing some immediacy and spice.

:-> :-) **Try This** :-O ;-)

Forward a Message to Another Writer   Sometimes you will want to pass along a message, either to give someone else information or to ask for his or her opinion. In this way, you can have a "conversation" about a topic and share opinions and ideas.

Look at your messages. Find one that you would like to share with someone. Usually, you can forward a message by pressing F, or command/alt F, and filling in the e-mail address of the person you want to send the message to. You can also add a message of your own to the original message. Perhaps you might want to ask the person you are sending the message to how he or she feels about the original message. Try this now. When you receive a response, examine the message closely. Does the person who received the forwarded message agree with you about the original message?

DEBATE AN ISSUE AND POST A THESIS

:-> :-) T r y   T h i s :-O ;-)

Debate an Issue and Post a Thesis   Use e-mail to build stronger arguments for your essays. Post your opinion on an arguable topic such as the legal age for drinking or the abuse of athletic scholarships and play devil's advocate with your classmates or correspondents. Ask them to attack your opinions as strongly as possible. You should then be forced to offer proof of your reasons for believing as you do. *After some online debate, form a thesis that takes a strong stand. Your thesis should be as specific as possible.* For example, you will probably not simply want to take a stand for or against capital punishment; that stance is much too broad. But you might want to say that you are for (or against) capital punishment for first-time offenders in murder cases. State the reasons why you think, feel, or believe as you do. Ask your correspondents to role-play a particular audience; for example, people who are for (or against) capital punishment in any case. Then think of ways to challenge their opinions and beliefs. If you play devil's advocate, your essays should have a much stronger thesis and supports.

Sample E-mail Debate   Which messages contain specific points that will help students improve their essays? Which ones should have been challenged to go deeper—to develop their thoughts more? How many writers need to explore terms such as "diverse reader" or "trash" or "insecure" in order to refine their thinking?

The Assignment   To discover the power of on-line debate, first review your reader-response to Robert's essay on "Low Taste." Then write e-mail to the class on the following subject:

For a person to be truly "educated" he or she should read trash as well as high-brow materials.

Agree or disagree with this statement, citing illustrations and examples from your own experience.
    Press R to respond to this message, or command/alt R.

HOLLY'S RESPONSE: A DIFFERENT OUTLOOK

Date: Thu, 19 Sep 1996 10:13:24 -0400 (EDT)

From: Holly Ann Donofrio <donofrio@xyzu.edu>

To: EDickinson <EDickinson@xyzu.edu>

Cc: Andrea Faith Schenk <aschenk@xyzu.edu>,
          ENGL110-106@Xyzu.Edu

Subject: Re: ASSIGNMENT FOR 9/19 (IN CLASS)

I think that to be truly educated to everything that goes on in the
world, you must read all kinds of things from trashy books and
comic books to good novels. By reading many different materials
you can get a taste for other people's point of views and ideas. It
may open your eyes to things you may not have known much
about. Reading things you may not have normally read may open
your interests to new and different things that may not have mattered to you before. It can give you a different outlook and perspective on things around you.

RICH'S RESPONSE: WALDEN, SHAKESPEARE, AND THE NATIONAL ENQUIRER

Date: Thu, 19 Sep 1996 10:14:31 -0400 (EDT)

From: Richard Paul Cook <01483@xyzu.edu>

To: Andrea Faith Schenk <aschenk@xyzu.edu>

Cc: EDickinson <EDickinson@xyzu.edu>, ENGL110-106@xyzu.edu

Subject: Re: ASSIGNMENT FOR 9/19 (IN CLASS)

I believe that to be a well educated and truly well rounded person,
you do have to read all kinds of books. Just because a novel isn't as
deep or profound as *Walden* doesn't mean it's not good. Besides,
mystery and adventure novels have characters we can cheer for
and root against; rarely have I found myself cheering for a Shake-
spearean character. Today's novels (and even comic books) seem
more real and we should read them on that alone. And let's be
honest; most of us would rather read something in the checkout
line in a super market than *Romeo and Juliet* or the *Odyssey*.

SEVERAL STUDENTS RESPONDED TO ANDREA, WHO SAID THAT WE SHOULD READ ALL SORTS OF THINGS TO BE TRULY EDUCATED. HERE'S HEATHER'S RESPONSE:

Date: Thu, 19 Sep 1996 10:16:31 -0400 (EDT)

From: Heather D'Agostino <01611@xyzu.edu>

To: Andrea Faith Schenk <aschenk@xyzu.edu>

Cc: EDickinson <EDickinson@xyzu.edu>, ENGL110-106@xyzu.edu

Subject: Re: ASSIGNMENT FOR 9/19 (IN CLASS)

I agree with some points of Andrea's reaction on "Low Taste" found in POI. She states that one should read trash as well as high-brow material in order to be educated. This is true in my opinion; however I feel that there is a limit to the trash that we should read. There are certain magazines and books that are too trashy. In these cases there is no benefit to reading them. Also for me a murder novel is not the best stress releaser for me, but it does serve as good entertainment. Finally, I do not feel that reading *Romeo and Juliet* made me any more cultured. I did however find it to be entertaining.

DAVID COMMENTS ON READING AND CULTURE:

Date: Thu, 19 Sep 1996 10:22:27 -0400 (EDT)

From: David Mich Persoleo <dpersole@xyzu.edu>

To: Andrea Faith Schenk <aschenk@xyzu.edu>

Cc: EDickinson <EDickinson@xyzu.edu>, ENGL110-106@xyzu.edu

Subject: Re: ASSIGNMENT 9/19 IN CLASS

I agree only partially with Andrea because, nobody should ever tell you anything, especially what to read. This is because reading is such a huge influence on our culture, and if someone tells us all to read the same thing then we will all think the same way (maybe). No one should be able to control the way we think or how we act.

THEN ANDREA COMMENTS ON MYSTERIES, PULP FICTION, AND *THE GOOD EARTH:*

Date: Thu, 19 Sep 1996 10:18:29 -0400 (EDT)

From: Andrea Faith Schenk <aschenk@xyzu.edu>

To: EDickinson <EDickinson@xyzu.edu>

Cc: ENGL110-106@xyzu.edu

Subject: Re: ASSIGNMENT FOR 9/19 (IN CLASS)

I feel that mystery stories and pulp fiction relieve stress because they create an outlet, a way to escape reality. Other "high brow" books help people to become more educated and cultured because some books teach about other cultures like *The Good*

Earth, about poverty in China, and books like that. They teach history and culture.

KYLE TALKS ABOUT ISOLATING OURSELVES FROM THE REST OF THE HUMAN RACE:

Date: Thu, 19 Sep 1996 10:20:54 -0400 (EDT)

From: Kyle Jonathan Belz <00548@xyzu.edu>

To: EDickinson <EDickinson@xyzu.edu>

Cc: ENGL110-106@xyzu.edu

Subject: Re: ASSIGNMENT FOR 9/19 (IN CLASS)

Based on Robert's essay "On low Taste", I believe that all readers of good taste also enjoy pulp in at least one of its various forms. If someone were to read only high quality material and neglect pulp fiction, then they would isolate themselves from the rest of the human race. It is essential to enjoy low, as well as high literature, to gain a better understanding of the human experience.

TONY CITES PERSONAL EXPERIENCE:

Date: Thu, 19 Sep 1996 10:44:41 -0400 (EDT)

From: Anthony Fel Barbone <barbone@xyzu.edu>

To: Mary Raphael Heim <03120@xyzu.edu>

Cc: Lakshman <lakshman@xyzu.edu>, EDickinson <EDickinson@xyzu.edu>, ENGL110-106@xyzu.edu

Subject: Re: ASSIGNMENT FOR 9/19 (IN CLASS)

I disagree with Mary because I feel that reading a wide variety of literature has not made me grow as a person at all. I think if you're going to read you should read something you enjoy.

DAVID DISTINGUISHES BETWEEN TEXTBOOKS AND NOVELS:

Date: Thu, 19 Sep 1996 10:29:37 -0400 (EDT)

From: David Mich Persoleo <dpersole@xyzu.edu>

To: EDickinson <EDickinson@xyzu.edu>

Cc: Andrea Faith Schenk <aschenk@xyzu.edu>, ENGL110-106@xyzu.edu

Subject: Re: ASSIGNMENT FOR 9/19 (IN CLASS)

Roberts comments on a class of books and different sections of people. People can't really label other people because there is always a grey area that will include or exclude someone somewhere. Taking offense to the class generalization is a little hasty. He isn't making fun of anyone for reading a book, he is just classifying sci-fi books and text books (or whatever) differently. Text books are there to learn from while novels are meant for entertainment.

SUE RAISES A NEW ISSUE—MENTALLY UNSTABLE PEOPLE:

Date: Thu, 19 Sep 1996 10:30:13 -0400 (EDT)

From: Susan Kate Dumbauld <susied@xyzu.edu>

To: Holly Ann Donofrio <donofrio@xyzu.edu>

Cc: EDickinson <EDickinson@xyzu.edu>,
Andrea Faith Schenk <aschenk@xyzu.edu>,
ENGL110-106@xyzu.edu

Subject: Re: ASSIGNMENT FOR 9/19 (IN CLASS)

Holly,
I agree with you that reading different materials can open the door to new beginnings and new ideas. Although a mentally unstable person read a book about murder or suicide, they might not be able to distinguish the difference between fiction and reality. I do believe that everyone should read both literary works and trash.

NANCY ADDRESSES DIVERSITY:

Date: Thu, 19 Sep 1996 10:30:29 -0400 (EDT)

From: Nancy Eliz Matthews <nancymat@xyzu.edu>

To: David Mich Persoleo <dpersole@xyzu.edu>

Cc: Andrea Faith Schenk <aschenk@xyzu.edu>,

EDickinson <EDickinson@xyzu.edu>, ENGL110-106@xyzu.edu

Subject: Re: ASSIGNMENT 9/19 IN CLASS

Hi David. I agree totally with you, I think if some one does tell you what to do, say or read for that matter is not really smart to begin with. Our culture depends of the fact that everyone is different and if we weren't then we would have no diversity in our culture.

The e-mail debate encouraged students to think about different kinds of reading and different meanings of literacy. It also challenged them to sharpen their views on censorship and on some people's attempts to impose standards of literacy on the larger community. Many students used the debate to find a focus for their essays.

When you post your thesis and supports, ask others to challenge you. Ask them to attach your argument, so you can sharpen your ways of thinking about your topic.

CUT AND PASTE FROM CATALOGS AND DATABASES

:-> :-) Try This :-O ;-)

Use the Resource File in Your Writing   When you are ready to draft your essay, look back at your resource files. Can you find some brainstorms or correspondence from classmates to support your opinions? If so, you can cut and paste information from your e-mail files into your document. Be sure you credit the source. For example, if you use e-mail to support a point, your text should clearly indicate the fact that this is e-mail from a particular person on a particular date. Also, if you create a Works Cited page, you should list your e-mail correspondence there. See Appendix A for formats for online sources in citations. After you use the resource file, think about which kinds of resources were helpful and which were not. Write some notes to yourself about the kinds of things you want to save in the future. To help others think about resource files, share your notes with classmates and compare your experience to theirs. Was your experience different from your classmates' experience or similar?

:-> :-) Try This :-O ;-)

Incorporate Quotations   When you check your resource file, you may discover some direct quotes from correspondents that you want to use in your essay. If so, it is important to remember to get permission to use the quote. When people write e-mail, they often assume, unless they are notified to the contrary, that the correspondence is casual and not for publication. Often, they are writing without access to sources or to their data; sometimes their remarks are extremely frank or off the cuff. Therefore, it is considered good "Netiquette" to ask before using quotes. If you use quotes, *build bridges from your own text into the quote.* Set the context. Do not just throw a quote into your essay and expect your readers to fill in the gaps. Add some quotes to your essay. Then, read the essay aloud to see if the quotes fit smoothly into your text.

:-> :-) Try This :-O ;-)

Advanced Exercise: Cutting and Pasting from On-line Library Catalogs and Databases   With Windows 95 or Mac's System 7, you can cut and paste information into your e-mail and then into your essays. Consult your manual or ask for help if you are unsure how to cut and paste. Usually, you use the mouse and the Edit menu to mark the information you want to move. If you clip from online sources, *keep a careful record of where you got the information.* If you keep a record as you go along, it will be much easier to document your paper later. Try cutting and pasting now. Report your results and the process you used online or in a journal.

THE SHAPE OF THE SCREEN—THE SHAPE OF THE MESSAGE

E-mail writers need to remember that, like paper, the screen has a particular shape and size; and information needs to be organized effectively to make use of this new writing space.

Sometimes, writers new to e-mail compose online exactly the same as on paper. The results can be ineffective. For example, writers may use a long introduction or background to introduce their topic, thinking that readers will just keep moving to the next screen, the way they usually move down a page of information. But this is not always the case. In fact, many e-mail readers read the first screen of a message and then reply. They may not even read the second or third screens. Or, if they do, they may have trouble remembering what was said on later screens, since they return to the top of the message to reply.

:-> :-) **Try This** :-O ;-)

Evaluating Messages: Following are two e-mail messages, both written on the subject of athletic scholarships. Which message is easier to answer? Why? Share your response with your classmates, online or face-to-face.

MESSAGE #1: SUBJECT: ATHLETIC SCHOLARSHIPS

Some people think that athletes should be treated differently from other students, but I don't think so. My roommate is a football player, and he says he is too busy playing sports to study. But I know that he spends a lot of time watching TV and talking to his friends. I also know that he doesn't take college seriously because he thinks he is going to play professional ball. But everyone knows that the chances of a college athlete making any money in professional sports are remote. Most college athletes end up flunking out of school and working in a fast-food place or some store at the mall. What do you think of this situation?

MESSAGE #2: SUBJECT: ATHLETIC SCHOLARSHIPS

I think athletic scholarships should be maintained, but they should be awarded to students in all sports (not just football and basketball) who demonstrate serious commitment to academics. Athletic scholarships, just like music or art scholarships, should be given for demonstrated excellence.

They should also be reviewed each year to see if the student athlete has maintained a satisfactory GPA. What do *you* think?

Although it is possible for readers to respond interlinearly (between the lines) of a message, point by point, many people prefer to write a response of a paragraph or so; therefore, they are likely to respond to the first part of the message, forgetting the later parts.

It is important to realize that e-mail calls for new ways of organizing information. Think in terms of being *con*cise and *pre*cise, avoiding "talky" writing (unless the audience and purpose are informal), and "chunking" information in a screenful. If you must write a long message, put an outline of the message at the beginning to indicate the contents. Observe the rules of Netiquette. Use subject lines effectively to preview the contents of a message. Avoid emotional outbursts. Use emoticons only where appropriate, and provide the necessary information for readers to reach you by phone, e-mail, and "snail mail" in a signature file.

< @ >   :-)   :- **YOUR ONLINE SELF** ;-O   :->   :-<

B e yourself, online, but be your *best* self. Just as you would talk differently to a boss than to a friend in person or on the phone, on the Net it is important to be able to express yourself both formally and informally. To become an effective e-mail communicator, try playing with several voices.

FINDING A VOICE

The following exercises will give you practice revising e-mail messages and trying on various personalities and attitudes to find your most powerful voice. Take the time to do each exercise carefully. If you master these skills, you will be an effective e-mail writer.

Be Concise   Because e-mail messages need to carry their meaning concisely, usually in one or two screenfuls, *practice summarizing your thoughts* and boiling down the information to its essence.

:->   :-) **Try This** :-O ;-)

Revise a Wordy Message   Read the following rambling e-mail message. Eliminate the unnecessary information and rewrite the message in one paragraph.

To: debate@utexas.edu

From: wordy@unewt.edu

Subject: SATs: Scholastic Aptitude Torture!

Many people feel that SATs do not show a good measure of a student's ability, but no one seems to be doing anything about the problem.

The SAT ordeal has been in existence for many years. All of us can remember entering the cold classroom on a Saturday morning during our senior year in high school with the sweat pouring off of our bodies. We were all slightly hung-over from the night before, and all of us were extremely nervous because we knew that much was at stake from the impending six-hour ordeal. We tried to joke, but none of us really felt like laughing. We worried if we had enough pencils with us. What if the point broke? Would we be allowed to sharpen it? We worried about what would happen if we had to go to the bathroom. Would the person supervising the exam allow us out of the room and back in again?

We got the booklet, which was taped shut, and sat poised to open it at the word "Go." We ripped open the seal and sighed as we looked at the length of the thing and at all of the parts with all of the warning messages about DO NOT GO ON! Or "Do the ones you know first." What if we didn't know anything??

Somehow, we managed to finish the thing—usually by marking in boxes at random on the answer sheet. Then we sweat for three more months until the envelopes came in the mail with the magic numbers in them. If we scored above 800, we were home free for most schools. Below 800, we had to listen to anxious or angry parents who had to explain to their friends why their child did not score well (he was tired that day, or he had the flu). We also had to endure their accusatory looks: why are you doing this to me—I have sacrificed everything for you!

Now, twenty years later, it is time for our children to take this same test. And what has been done about it? Nothing!

It is time to propose a solution to this problem. Possible solutions might be to ask schools to accept a portfolio of work or to ask them to do personal interviews of students who want to attend their school. Anything is better than the meaningless sweat-a-thon we went through.

Condense the message above into one screenful (about 22 lines, and put the call for action where it will be seen.

Being _Precise_ (Addresses and So Forth)   Because e-mail messages are so distilled, it is especially important to have your facts straight. What will the reader(s) want to know? Probably, they need to know times, dates, places, names, steps in a process, etc. *Before sending a message, ask yourself, "Am I giving the reader the information he or she needs to know in order to respond to my message or to act on it?"*

:-> :-) **T r y T h i s** :-O ;-)

Revise a Vague Message
The following e-mail message is vague. It also lacks crucial details. Rewrite the message so that the intended reader will be able to respond or act on the information.

> To: students@badgeru.edu
>
> From: faculty@badgeru.edu
>
> Subject: Choosing a Major

> Entering students should choose a major as soon as possible. If you are confused about a major, consult the *Student Guide to Policies,* which is available in many campus offices. Or, talk to a member of the faculty. After you have decided which major you prefer, fill out the form and submit it.

"Talky" Writing   Because e-mail is such an informal medium, writing often becomes conversational or "talky." Such a style is appropriate when you are writing to friends or classmates, but sometimes, especially when writing to teachers, bosses, or international audiences, you may need to use a more formal style.

FINDING AN AUDIENCE AND A PURPOSE

As with any kind of writing, you should always consider your *subject, audience, and purpose.* Perhaps your teacher or boss calls herself *Barbie* online, but are you sure she really wants *you* to call her that name? When in doubt, try being the same sort of self online that you would be if you visited this person in her office. Power relationships such as those between students and teachers can change online, but it's usually safest to let the teacher call the tone. Watch for signals.

:-> :-) **T r y T h i s** :-O ;-)

Matching the Tone   The following set of e-mail messages was exchanged between a student and a teacher. In this exchange, the student assumed that the teacher wanted to have a buddy-buddy relationship, but she did not. First, identify the clues in the teacher's messages that show clearly that she wanted to maintain a formal classroom relationship online. Then rewrite the student's messages to adjust to the tone the teacher expected.

From: iamastudent@anyschool.edu

To: myteacher@anyschool.edu

Subject: missed classes

> Anne,
> Sorry I had to miss class all last week. Something came up and it took longer than I expected.
> See you. John

From: myteacher@anyschool.edu

To: iamastudent@anyschool.edu

Subject: Missed Classes

> John,
> My office hours are M-W from 9–12. You should call x2934 and make an appointment to come in and talk about the missed classes and plan to make up the work. I hope things improve for you soon.
> Professor Larson

From: iamastudent@anyschool.edu

To: myteacher@anyschool.edu

Subject: missed classes

> Anne, I'm really busy this week. I'll give you a call next week and see if you can give me an appointment that fits my schedule.
> P.S. Did I really miss anything?

"Chunking" Information   If you need to write a long message on occasion, you will want to learn how to "chunk" information into screenfuls. *You cannot assume that the reader will scroll back and forth to check details.* Reading on a screen is much different from reading on paper, where readers can flip pages and look forward and backward easily. Therefore, *each screenful should be able to stand alone.*

:-> :-) **Try This** :-O ;-)

Change a Paper-Format Message to a Screen Format   In the following e-mail message, because the writer has followed the kind of format best suited to paper correspondence, it is difficult for online readers to follow the information. First, read the message carefully. Then revise it so that each screenful can stand alone.

Date: Thu, 16 Nov 1995 10:26:09 -0500 (EST)

From: John Pe Panteleakis <90482@xyzu.edu>

To: engl110-106@brahms.xyzu.edu

Cc: EDickinson <EDickinson@brahms.xyzu.edu>

Subject: Women in Japan—progress on research paper

A term paper is no walk through the park. It takes time, thinking, and most importantly, research. In order to write a good paper, one has to manage his time well, know what he wants to do, and do the research necessary to back the points that he wants to make.

My research paper has been both frustrating and finally productive. At first my topic was on the treatment of elderly in other societies. My first mistake in finding information on this topic was procrastinating on getting to the library. I could find hardly anything that would be useful for my paper. Then, I was stuck on to what I could change my topic to next. Almost all of the recent material on homelessness had already been taken out and the idea of using rape as a topic came up but there are too many aspects of it to choose just one.

Finally, when I was at the brink on going crazy, I decided to try just one more topic, the advancement of women in Japan. I have found about 5 usable sources on it but some of them say the same things. One source in particular has given me many ideas about what I want to get across in my paper. It tells about the burdens of being a woman in Japan, such as discrimination and inequality, responsibilities, and advancements that they have made.

I have made great progress on my paper as of now. My main strategy to make progress was to write one page of notes and ideas a day until I felt that I had enough to begin typing and putting my ideas together. I have gotten half way through the paper and still have a few more sources to explore. This topic can be related to the struggle that the women of America have gone through and made progress and are still making process. The women's progress in Japan is about a few decades behind than that in America.

The next time I have a research paper assigned, I will go to the library as soon as possible just to be sure I get the material I need for my topic. Also, I want to have a better and clearer idea of what I want to write about before I start the actual writing.

"Netiquette" The Internet, especially e-mail, is a wild and woolly space for writing where the rules are still evolving; therefore, it is important that all writers follow some common courtesies. For example, if you receive a private message, do not forward it unless doing so will *not* injure the original writer. If you quote from e-mail, do it accurately and by permission of the original writer—especially if you plan to publish the material. When writing messages, don't use the Caps Lock key because it appears that YOU ARE SHOUTING! Be wary of using lots of exclamation points or question marks. This, too, looks like an attempt to dominate a discussion. Of course, there should be no name calling and insults online. You are known only by your words. If you insult people, you will look like an idiot.

:-> :-) **Try This** :-O ;-)

Revise an Offensive Message The following message is offensive. The writer is trying to convince others to adopt his point of view on a subject where there is much disagreement, but he manages only to sound strident and unconvincing. Revise the message so that it is assertive without being offensive.

OFFENSIVE MESSAGE

To: class@commcoll.edu

From: iamstupid@nuttyu.edu

Re: tv violence

Harold said tv does no harm. Obviously, he doesn't read the newspapers. Any jerk knows that kids who watch too much tv—especially violent shows—is much more likely to hit you over the head than the kid who plays with Barbie dolls!

"Flaming" Sometimes online discussions get really hot. If, for example, a person is called racial epithets or is labeled a liar, e-mail discussions can quickly degenerate into war zones. If you receive a message that seems insulting, try not to respond in kind. Instead, *wait a bit and think about what the author said.* Then ask for clarification of certain issues, or respond with humor. Sometimes humor is the most effective way to douse a flame. Remember, the writer of the message might have been under great stress or time pressure when it was written. It used to be that letters sat on desks for days or weeks before they were answered. Now, most e-mail writers feel compelled to answer a message as soon as they receive it. Therefore, some messages are written more in heat than in reflection.

:-> :-) Try This :-O ;-)

Cool Down a Flame   Read the following e-mail exchange and note the hot nature of the discussion. Rewrite one of the messages to cool down the flames.

To: pharrigan@newstateU.edu

From: angryman@oldstateU.edu

Subject: glass ceiling

Paula,
I'm tired of hearing about the "glass ceiling." Everyone knows it's a fiction. These days, women can get anything they want. They just have to know what they want!

To: angryman@oldstateU.edu

From: pharrigan@newstateU.edu

Subject: glass ceiling

Harry,
Just because you have never bumped your head on the glass ceiling doesn't mean it doesn't exist! Just look at the administration at your school. I'm willing to bet it's mostly male and mostly white! Don't cast stones unless you want to hear some glass breaking at oldU!

To: pharrigan@newstateU.edu

From: angryman@oldstateU.edu

Subject: glass ceiling

Paula,
It's women like you who cause the problem! You're all heat and no light! Why don't you get a life instead of sitting around talking about glass ceilings! Bet you haven't had a date for years!

Emoticons   Because e-mail is a text-only medium, some writers like to include little drawings to show their mood or intent. For example, some writers like to include smiley faces such as :-), or sad faces such as :-(. Some readers love these "emoticons," but others are not amused. *Always consider your audience and purpose.*

:-> :-) Try This :-O ;-)

The following message contains several emoticons. Which seem appropriate? Which do not? Revise the message, eliminating inappropriate emoticons.

To: myboss@anycorp.com

From: employee@anycorp.com

Subject: Progress Report

> You asked for an update on my group's progress on the Johnson Project, and I am pleased to be able to supply one :-). So far, our group has had its ups and downs ;-). We were surprised to hear that Johnson may not be able to expand this project as they had planned :-O. But you may be aware of the possibility of a merger of Johnson and Johnson :->! If that is the case, the project may be tabled for an indefinite period of time :-(.

Signature Files   Many writers like to create signature files that are automatically appended to the end of any message they write. Usually these files contain the writer's name, "snail mail" (U.S. mail) address, and phone number. Sometimes writers add favorite quotes, witty sayings, or pictures drawn with letters and numbers. Signature files should be no more than four lines long. If you want to add a signature file to your mail messages, check with your computer support office on campus to find out how to create and append this file.

<@> :-) GOOD IMPRESSIONS :-O :-> :-<

Signature files represent you to the world.
   Think carefully before creating your file. Cute or sarcastic signature files can send the wrong message.

Acronyms   If you want to look like a seasoned e-mail writer (and if you want to be able to understand some rather cryptic messages), get acquainted with the abbreviations or acronyms common to e-mail. For example, in some messages you may see *BTW* (by the way), *FYI* (for your information), and

IMHO (in my humble opinion). If you join a listserv, a mass-mailing list to a group of people interested in a particular topic such as a rock celebrity, vegetarian cooking, or right-wing politics in a particular country (see Chapter 2), you are likely to see lots of acronyms used by list regulars or insiders. Often, there is a record of the lingo used in the discussions in a *FAQ* (frequently asked questions) file that you can obtain from the listserv. If you send a message to the group to ask the meaning of an acronym, you will look like a "newbie." But that's okay: everyone is a "newbie" at some time on the Net.

FINDING AN AUDIENCE AND A PURPOSE: PEN PALS ON THE WORLD WIDE WEB

All over the world, using e-mail, groups of people are finding a community on the Internet. Sometimes these groups fill a *local* purpose—putting people in touch with one another for social events or listing community resources for those in need. Other times they establish contact for people interested in national or even international causes or issues.

Listed below are examples of various e-mail communities. As an exercise in using e-mail to build a community of your own, write to a local group, a national group, and an international group.

FINDING PEN PALS

If you know how to use a search engine such as Yahoo!, AltaVista, or Webcrawler, you can search the World Wide Web to find e-mail addresses for groups from your local area or groups related to one of your national or international interests. If you do not yet know how to search the Web, you can find information on this subject in Chapter 4.

FINDING E-MAIL ADDRESSES IN ONLINE DIRECTORIES

Casting a Broad Net: Wide Searches   The best strategy for online searches is to combine terms using *and* (a Boolean operator). For example: A search performed on November 15, 1996, on AltaVista using the keywords *students and email* gave the following results:

SITES FOR PARTICULAR SCHOOLS

E-Mail Directory. Please type in a search string to identify a student or staff member's username. Type in either first or last name. Usernames normally . . . http://orion.bercol.bm/cgi-bin/student_list—size 339 bytes—27 Jun 96

IOWA CENTRAL STUDENTS EMAIL ACCOUNTS

Iowa Central Student Email Accounts. Below is a list of Email accounts for students who have elected to apply for an account at Iowa Central Community . . . http://elvis.iccc.cc.ia.us:8000/WWW/CATALOG/STUDENT.htm—size 7K—25 Jun 96

SITES WHERE YOU CAN FIND ADDRESSES OF INTERNATIONAL STUDENTS:

Students Using Email to Communicate Internationally [Prev][Next][Index] Students Using Email to Communicate Internationally. To: echalk@cleo.murdoch.edu.au. Subject: Students Using Email to Communicate . . . http://www.citybeach.wa.edu.au/mailarchive3/echalk.9501/msg00044.html—size 6K—31 Jan 95

Finding More Specific Information: Narrowing Your Search   When you add still more information to the search terms—for example, the geographical area where you are trying to locate addresses—you can get even more specific information. For example, a search for *students and e-mail and Texas* turned up the following results.

1. PSYCHOLOGY GRADUATE STUDENTS AT TEXAS A&M

The following is a directory of the graduate students in the psychology department. You may follow the links to more information; including area . . . http://www.tamu.edu/psyc/grads.html—size 6K—21-May-97—English

2. LOANS TO HIGHER EDUCATION STUDENTS IN TEXAS

Loans to Higher Education Students in Texas. Loans to higher education students in Texas have grown both from state and federal fund sources. Projections . . . http://www.lbb.state.tx.us/lbb/members/reports/summary/HELOANS.htm—size 4K—24-May-97—English

3. GRANTS TO HIGHER EDUCATION STUDENTS IN TEXAS

Grants to Higher Education Students in Texas. After a period of rapid growth in grants to higher education students, grant are projected to remain . . . http://www.lbb.state.tx.us/lbb/members/reports/summary/HEGRANTS.htm—size 3K—24-May-97—English

4. FOUR TAMU-CC STUDENTS GARNER TEXAS FAMILY BUSINESS ASSOCIATION AND FOUNDATION SCHOLARSHIPS

The Texas Family Business Association and Foundation has . . . http://www.tamucc.edu/~pioweb/news/4aug95/fambusch.htm—size 2K—25-May-97—English

5. STUDENTS AT TEXAS TECH UNIVERSITY

Students at Texas Tech University. A B C D E F G H I J K L M N O P Q R S T V W X Y Z. There are 442 home pages here. A. abdelgawad, ayman—taasa, last . . . http://pegasus.acs.ttu.edu/personal_hp.html—size 59K—24-May-97

6. PHYSICS GRADUATE STUDENTS—TEXAS A&M UNIVERSITY

Graduate Students. This list is current as of September 28, 1995. Please send corrections to wwwadmin@chaos.tamu.edu.
Thanks! [A | B | C | D | E | F | G . . .
http://physics.tamu.edu/students/students.html—size 21K—25-May-97—English

7. STUDENTS AT TEXAS TECH UNIVERSITY

Students at Texas Tech University. A B C D E F G H I J K L M N O P Q R S T V W X Y Z. There are 440 home pages here. A. abdelgawad, ayman—taasa, last . . . http://www.ttu.edu/personal_hp.html—size 59K—2-May-97

8. STUDENTS FROM TEXAS

http://guweb.georgetown.edu/admissions/student/states/tx.html—size 5K—24-Oct-96—English

9. CHI—SAN ANTONIO AND SOUTH TEXAS STUDENTS

CHI's San Antonio and South Texas Students. Alajandro from Colombia playing the piano at a recent party. Kristjan Laube (Estonia) contacting his family at http://www.chinet.org/regions/az_r5c/sananton.html—size 3K—17-May-97—English

10. FINANCIAL AID FOR TEXAS STUDENTS

http://www.thecb.state.tx.us/divisions/student/finaid/finmain.htm—size 215 bytes—7-Mar-97—English

> FINDING INFORMATION ABOUT YOUR COMMUNITY <

If you search the Web using terms such as *students and email and* (the name of your local community or state), you are likely to find a treasure trove of sites to visit that will include e-mail addresses for government, community, and recreational leaders. Try searching your area. You may discover a wealth of interesting resources.

STATE OF TEXAS EMAIL INFORMATION

State of Texas: Government Information. Contacting State Officials. Governor. Elected Officials. State Senators and Representatives. Policy on Email . . . http://www.texas.gov/email.html—size 2K—6 May 96

TEST YOUR EMAIL ADDRESS ON THE TEXAS MARKETPLACE

Test Your EMail Address on the Texas Marketplace. Check your registered E-MAIL address. Quite a few of the EMail addresses registered with the Texas . . . http://www.texas-one.org/market/testmail.htm—size 2K—4 Jun 96

INTERNET TEXAS PEOPLE, COMPANY AND EMAIL FINDERS

People, Company, and Email Finders. Internet Address Finder. Who Where? Four11 White Page Directory. Switchboard—Telephone Numbers & Addresses. The . . . http://www.itexas.net/public/finders.htm—size 1K—18 May 96

E-MAIL FORM—FIRST TEXAS HONDA

First Texas Honda
http://www.firsttexashonda.com/eMailHonda.html—size 3K—16 May 96

TEXAS STATE COMPTROLLER E-MAIL

E-mail: www@www.cpa.state.tx.us. Note: This is an HTML form. You must have a browser that supports forms in order to use it. If you do not see text editing . . . http://www.cpa.texas.gov/www.html—size 1K—27 Feb 96

TEXAS INTERNET PEOPLE, COMPANY AND E-MAIL FINDERS

People, Company, and E-mail Finders. Internet Address Finder. Who Where? Four11 White Page Directory. Switchboard—Telephone Numbers & Addresses. The . . . http://www.texinet.net/finders.htm—size 1K—7 May 96

GENERATED E-MAIL FORM FOR EAST TEXAS WANT ADS

EAST TEXAS. WANT ADS. Personal ads can be placed here for $3.95 for 10 words, and run for one month. $.99 for additional 10 words, and you can have your . . . http://www.pcsc.net/wantads/wasubmit.htm—size 2K—3 Feb 96

GENERATED E-MAIL FORM FOR EAST TEXAS EMAIL WHITE PAGES

EAST TEXAS EMAIL. WHITE PAGES. NAME. CITY. ADDRESS. MASS MAIL. Adam Graser. Irving. agraser@airmail.net. No. Alan Fannin. Hawkins. afannin@tyler.net. . . . http://www.pcsc.net/e-texas/emaillst.htm—size 10K—12 Jun 96

Notice that this list does *not* give students' addresses, but it does give some interesting information. If you want to find students' addresses, a good strategy would be to search for the home page for the school on the Web and select the e-mail directory for students. For example, I found the e-mail directory for the University of Texas at Austin by typing the name of the school as a search term in AltaVista. You can also find students' e-mail addresses by searching Gopher. Ask your instructor for specific directions.

LISTSERVS: TAKING A STAND

LISTSERVS DEFINED

Listservs are mass mailings online. Subscribers join a list so that they can participate in a discussion with others interested in the same subjects. There are *listservs* for every conceivable subject including fitness, politics, the environment, classical music, rock music, cooking, gardening, classic cars, and even writing. When a writer sends a note to the list, all subscribers get a copy. Lists help people distribute information, collaborate on a project, make plans, and argue or discuss issues of importance.

PARTICIPATING IN A CLASS LIST

Your first experience with lists might be local; that is, you might participate in a discussion list with others in your class. If your teacher has set up a class list, you will be able to send messages to the whole class and to read messages that other students have posted in a public space rather like a bulletin board, except more interactive. On a typical community bulletin board (in a supermarket, for example) people post messages selling things, looking for jobs, asking for help for a specific problem, or looking for someone to talk to. Someone walking by sees the message, writes down the phone number, and goes home to pick up a phone and call. Perhaps the caller reaches an answering machine! In any case, the usual type of bulletin board is a one-to-one type of communication, but lists provide much more opportunity for many people to connect to each other.

Joining in a discussion on a class list can help you to find a voice. First, it's a "safe" space to voice an opinion. Usually, your classmates will be tolerant of your views. Everyone is learning how to use the list and how to adjust to college life, so no one is likely to get terribly offended if you offer a surprising or strong opinion. In fact, classmates will probably welcome it as a real change from the predictable views often expressed in classrooms. If you venture to offer a *real* opinion—something you truly believe, think, and feel (not something the teacher "expects" to hear), your voice will begin to grow strong. If classmates disagree with you, they will need to use *words and illustrations and examples* to prove their point. They won't able to get their way simply because they are more outgoing in the classroom or because the teacher happens to look in their direction more often. Using a listserv, everyone is on equal ground. Appearance doesn't count: no one cares what kinds of clothes you are wearing or if you are having a "bad hair" day.

If you send mail to the class list, you should use the *list's address*, not the address of individuals on the list. For example, students in my first-year writing course participate in a class list by sending a message to ENGL110-106@xyzU.edu. If they send to that address, everyone in the class gets a copy of the message. If students want to respond to one of these messages, using Pine and many other brands of e-mail software, they have the option of replying just to the sender or to the whole class. Sometimes it take a little while for students to realize that if they choose to reply to all recipients, *everyone* sees their note. At first, the public nature of the discussion can be unsettling. But soon everyone joins in. Often, things that are never said in the regular classroom get said online since students have a chance to think over their remarks. They may feel more comfortable commenting on some else's remark because of the relatively level playing field of the screen.

Posting to the class list can also help you to improve your offline writing. For example, if you plan your argument papers online, you can get help from your classmates. You will improve your writing because you will be forced to compress your ideas—to make them fit into the space of a screen; therefore, you will begin to refine your argument and clarify your thinking. You will become aware of writing for real people—not just for a teacher. Writing is both an art and a skill, like playing the violin or painting a picture: the more you write, the more fluent you will become. So put your thoughts into writing early and often and watch your work take shape online.

PARTICIPATING IN A CLASS LISTSERV

:-> :-) Try This :-O ;-)

Send a Message to Your Class Listserv   Check with your teacher to find out the address. Once you have established contact with the list, you will soon find plenty of occasions to post replies to messages or to ask for help with your writing. The important thing is to establish contact and *maintain it.* Get started now!

Posting a Thesis and Supports   When you write an argument paper (in a sense, all papers are argument papers in that you are trying to persuade someone of the rightness of your views on a subject), remember that you should *not* just write a report (for example, Everything You Wanted to Know

About AIDS But Were Afraid to Ask). Rather, you should think through a narrowly focused part of your topic and take a stand—form a *thesis.*

A thesis sticks its neck out. A thesis makes a statement that somebody could disagree with. For example, no one would disagree with a statement that AIDS is a terrible disease, but someone could disagree if you chose to make a thesis about the treatment of AIDS or the government funding of AIDS research. For example, you might argue that the best treatment for AIDS is some new drug therapy, or a combination of a natural food diet and rest. You might also argue for or against the proposition that the U.S. government should increase spending on AIDS research, depending on your position on the responsibility of the government to fund research into diseases that may be transmitted (in some instances) by lifestyle.

If you post your tentative thesis and supports on a class list, classmates can help you sharpen your focus. Following is an example of an online discussion that helped a student take a firmer stand on her topic:

ANDREA, FEELING UNMOTIVATED TO BEGIN DRAFTING HER PAPER, POSTS A GENERAL TOPIC AND ASKS FOR THE CLASS'S OPINION:

Date: Thu, 14 Nov 1996 09:55:20 -0500 (EST)

From: Andrea Faith Schenk <aschenk@xyzu.edu>

To: ENGL110-106@xyzu.edu

Cc: EDickinson <EDickinson@amherst.edu>

Subject: Women and How they are portrayed in Magazine Ads

Hi everyone, I'm doing my paper on how women are portrayed in Magazine ads. I have a lot of information, and now all I have to do is sit down and actually write the paper. What do you all think? Do you think that women are portrayed in a degrading manner? Or, do you think that they are shown in a realistic point of view? Andrea

Then Kristy follows with specific examples from the media to reinforce Andrea's attitude. Although Kristy was actually replying to a message from another student, Mary, her examples helped Andrea. Kristy also volunteers to share some firsthand experiences privately.

Date: Thu, 14 Nov 1996 10:10:01 -0500 (EST)

From: Kristy Lynn Redford <klr@xyzu.edu>

To: Mary Raphael Heim <03120@xyzu.edu>

Cc: EDickinson <EDickinson@amherst.edu>

Subject: Re: eating disorders in teenagers

I think the media's portrayal of women has a big effect on teenagers, especially females. Because there isn't an overabundance of female role models for girls like there is for males, most girls look to "famous" women, such as models or actresses. Models (like Kate Moss) are generally one body type, skinny. Young girls especially see men's reaction to these models and automatically equate this body type with "sexiness." In general women are looked down upon if they are overweight; males generally are not. Weight presents more of a self-esteem issue for females. If you need any more ideas, let me know. I've had some first-hand experience in dealing with an anoretic friend.

THEN JENNIFER EXPANDS THE DISCUSSION BY REDEFINING THE MEDIA'S PORTRAYAL OF WOMEN AS "GODDESSES" AND TALKS ABOUT THE PRESSURE ON SOME WOMEN TO STRIVE TO EMULATE THESE GODDESSES:

From: Jennifer E McKinley <jennymc@xyzu.edu>

To: Andrea Faith Schenk <aschenk@xyzu.edu>

Cc: ENGL110-106@xyzu.edu, EDickinson <EDickinson@amherst.edu>

Subject: Re: Women and How they are portrayed in Magazine Ads

I think women are portrayed in a very unrealistic manner. How many women actually look "perfect"? No-one. Magazines portray women as though they are goddesses and encourage their readers to strive for "the look". I feel that is degrading to women because it make them feel as though they have to look like a toothpick or something pretty close to that in order to be beautiful. I don't feel that way personally, but I know that a lot of my friends feel as though they are too fat, too this, or too that and it's sad because it's not true. They see what is portrayed in a magazine and think they have to live up to that. For some that can become an obsession that could kill them (anorexia, bulimia, etc.). I hope this helped you some.
Jen

TONY QUESTIONS JENNIFER'S POINT OF VIEW:

From: Anthony Fel Barbone <barbone@xyzu.edu>

To: Jennifer E McKinley <jennymc@xyzu.edu>

Cc: Andrea Faith Schenk <aschenk@xyzu.edu>, ENGL110-106@xyzu.edu,

EDickinson <EDickinson@amherst.edu>

Subject: Re: Women and How they are portrayed in Magazine Ads

I don't think the women are shown in a degrading manner. Not because I'm a guy, but because that's what they want to do. They are getting paid good money for what they want to do, so it's not degrading at all.

JENNIFER, BEGINNING TO FIND HER VOICE AND A THESIS AS WELL, REPLIES TO TONY:

Date: Thu, 14 Nov 1996 10:36:14 -0500 (EST)

From: Jennifer E McKinley <jennymc@xyzu.edu>

To: Anthony Fel Barbone <barbone@xyzu.edu>

Cc: Andrea Faith Schenk <aschenk@xyzu.edu>,
ENGL110-106@xyzu.edu,
EDickinson <EDickinson@amherst.edu>

Subject: Re: Women and How they are portrayed in Magazine Ads

I guess I wouldn't say that it is degrading to women because women are doing the job, but I do think that it causes women with a low self esteem to feel as though they have to have the "look" of the 90's. How many women actually look like that? Yes they are beautiful, but why not include average beautiful women? I think seeing a more realistic portrayal of women would discourage readers from feeling as though they are not beautiful because they are not thin and tall and do not have the "perfect body".

THEN ANDREA THANKS JENNIFER FOR HER HELP (BOTH STUDENTS ENDED UP WRITING ON THIS TOPIC):

Date: Thu, 14 Nov 1996 10:42:26 -0500 (EST)

From: Andrea Faith Schenk <aschenk@xyzu.edu>

To: Jennifer E McKinley <jennymc@xyzu.edu>

Cc: ENGL110-106@xyzu.edu, EDickinson
<EDickinson@amherst.edu>

Subject: Re: Women and How they are portrayed in Magazine Ads

I guess that you're right, they are really portrayed poorly. Women are seen as sex objects in a lot of these ads and I think that needs to be changed. Thanks for your help!
Andrea

TONY PRESSES HIS POINT:

From: Anthony Fel Barbone <barbone@xyzu.edu>

To: EDickinson@amherst.edu <EDickinson@amherst.edu@>

Cc: Jennifer E McKinley <jennymc@xyzu.edu>,
Andrea Faith Schenk <aschenk@xyzu.edu>,
ENGL110-106@xyzu.edu,

EDickinson <EDickinson@amherst.edu>

Subject: Re: Women and How they are portrayed in Magazine Ads

Jen, only *some* women are bulemic and anoretic that are in those pictures. Also, some women do look perfect.

NOW JENNIFER SPEAKS ELOQUENTLY ABOUT HER TOPIC. SHE'S READY TO WRITE. SHE HAS HER THESIS!

Date: Thu, 14 Nov 1996 18:01:12 -0500 (EST)

From: Jennifer E McKinley <jennymc@xyzu.edu>

To: Anthony Fel Barbone <barbone@xyzu.edu>

Cc: EDickinson@amherst.edu <EDickinson@amherst.edu@>,
Andrea Faith Schenk <aschenk@xyzu.edu>, ENGL110-
106@xyzu.edu, EDickinson <EDickinson@amherst.edu>

Subject: Re: Women and How they are portrayed in Magazine Ads

Tony,
I wasn't talking about the women in the ads . . . I was talking about the effect it can have on readers. A few of my friends found themselves starving themselves so they would look like the models in the magazines. That's not healthy and it could have led them, as it has led many, to an eating disorder. Society puts too much emphasis on looking like the models. They are very fortunate to have bodies like that; unfortunately, not all of us are "naturally perfect" and it has caused many women to starve themselves in hope that they would end up looking like the models.

Challenged to define and articulate her point of view, Jennifer has clarified her thinking and found motivation to write a strong paper on a topic that mattered to her. Because of her online debate, she found a voice and conviction.

:-> :-) T r y T h i s :-O ;-)

To Improve Your Academic Writing, Take a Stand   Post a strong opinion to your classmates on a topic of your choice and list your reasons for believing, thinking, or feeling the way you do. Ask your classmates to challenge your statements—to find holes in your logic. When they challenge you, ask them to go deeper. Respond to what they say. Chances are your thinking will become clearer and your position stronger.

Usually, everyone participates more or less equally in the online discussions about topics, but sometimes one or two students dominate the discourse. Once in a while everyone else is willing to stand back and let two or three students debate a controversial issue hotly: the rest of the students join in when they see a point to be made. For example, two students in one of my classes debated the merits of *The Bell Curve*, by Richard J. Herrnstein—a controversial book about the possible relationship between race and IQ scores on standardized tests. John (not his real name) was in favor of the book; Katie (not her real name) was against it. Because each student challenged the other to defend his or her statements in full view of the rest of the class, both students wrote fine papers. Both students were challenged in an online debate to back up their arguments with concrete illustrations and examples, and both were confronted with opposing viewpoints. So when they drafted the final versions of their essays, they could anticipate the objections of their audience and avoid logical fallacies such as begging the question.

It is impossible to include their entire debate (which ran to fourteen messages and nearly forty pages of text), but following are the first two messages in which they set up their opposing points of view and listed their major points. Both students did a fine job of taking a stand.

Date:	Thu, 17 Nov 1994 16:02:31 -0500 (EST)
From:	John Sezzo <sezzo@brahms.xyzu.edu>
To:	EDickinson <EDickinson@amherst.edu@brahms.xyzu.edu>
Cc:	ENGL110-106@xyzu.edu
Subject:	Re: The heredity of intelligence

The lead story for the Review [a student newspaper] on November 4 concerned the new book The Bell Curve: Intelligence and Class Structure In American Life. The book brings back the ever unpopular idea that intelligence can be inherited.

The book has sparked some lively debate among the press and the authors have been called everything from "Neo-Nazi's" to "Courageous men . . ."

Do you believe genes or the environment are more important factors of intelligence?

Do you believe the "liberal" media is unwilling to accept an idea as politically incorrect and demoralizing (maybe even Un-American) as inherited intelligence?

The controversy surrounding The Bell Curve stems mostly from one chapter which stated that when the environments were equalized, the East Asians scored 3 pts. higher on the average than whites and African Americans scored 15 pts lower than whites. Comments?

You may reply to me alone (for uncompromised privacy) or post to the group.

Please respond. I NEED YOUR HELP.

"Ain't no time to hate. . . ."

Date:	Fri, 18 Nov 1994 12:59:07 -0500 (EST)
From:	Katie Lokker <katie@strauss.xyzu.edu>
To:	John Sezzo <sezzo@brahms.xyzu.edu>
cc:	EDickinson <EDickinson@amherst.edu
Subject:	Re: The heredity of intelligence

Hey John!
I think that you came in for your conference just after mine. Anyway, here goes.
On Thu, 17 Nov 1994, John Sezzo wrote:
> The lead story for the Review on November 4 concerned the
> new book The Bell Curve: Intelligence and Class Structure
> In American Life. The book brings back the ever unpopular
> idea that intelligence can be inherited. The book has sparked
> some lively debate among the press and the authors
Yup.
> have been called everything from "Neo-Nazi's" to "Courageous
> men . . . " Do you believe genes or the environment are more
> important factors of intelligence?
The two cannot be separated.
> Do you believe the "liberal" media is unwilling to accept an
> idea as politically incorrect and demoralizing (maybe even
> Un-American) as inherited intelligence?
Inherited intelligence, yes. (Intelligence can be thought of as just another characteristic—the trouble comes in measuring it) Racial inherited intelligence, no. If you pause here and think why this might be, the reason shows. If racial inherited intelligence is accepted as a given—we suddenly don't ever need to be scientific

or to test the hypothesis again, just look at the person's skin, treat and educate them accordingly then . . . Just get rid of those who cause the downfall of society (you know—the poor downtrodden masses).

Suddenly not to help the building of another Auschwitz is Un-American, suddenly not to help to build an Auschwitz makes you one of the ones that causes the downfall of society.

> The controversy surrounding The Bell Curve stems mostly from
> one chapter which stated that when the environments were
> equalized, the East Asians scored 3 pts. higher on the average
> than whites and African Americans scored 15 pts lower than
> whites. Comments?

Don't you think you should ask someone Asian instead? Just kidding?

Donno. I'll be reading this book for my paper too. Off the cuff, my comment is that to separate the social factors and income from consideration is to misrepresent, and misreport. Also you should remember that the East Asians are a pretty select group. We closed immigration to 1790 proportions for a while, and the only ones allowed in were those who would help us (since immigrants can't offer money usually) via muscle power or brain power . . .

:-> :-) Try This :-O ;-)

Write Responses to John and Katie to Challenge Some of Their Major Points   Ask them to examine their presuppositions or beliefs. Look for holes in their logic. Challenge them to think more deeply about the possibility of the inheritance of IQ.

Debating Topics   Post your own thesis and supports and invite your classmates to debate with you. Ask them to take the other side of the issue and list all of their reasons for disagreeing with you—even if they secretly agree. In fact, the more they disagree with you the better. (See Chapter 1 for a sample of a simple version of debating topics.)

:-> :-) Try This :-O ;-)

Invite Your Classmates to Play Devil's Advocate   In this case, class members go a step further than simply disagreeing with you; instead, they *attack* your logic, finding holes anywhere they can, so that you can attack back. When playing devil's advocate, it's important to remember that it's not fair to attack the *person* writing—only the argument. So that everyone plays by the same rules, the class should start off by generating a list of acceptable and nonacceptable kinds of attacks on arguments.

Sharing Resources　In the sample class debate, some of the writers suggested sources of help such as other students in the dorm or illustrations and examples; other students suggested sources on the WWW or in the library. If students support each other in this way, writing becomes much easier for everyone—*and* more interesting.

:-> :-) **Try This** :-O ;-)

Post a Topic and a Tentative Thesis and Supports and Ask Classmates for Help Locating a Specific Source　You might want help finding a particular book or Web site or local information or resources such as the Office of Women's Affairs or the dean of students. Students should help each other brainstorm for possible sources for papers. In doing this, you will learn to think broadly and deeply about possible sources for papers and to support a community of writers.

Helping Other Writers　There is an art to making helpful comments to other writers. If you are too polite, you won't be helpful at all. If you are insulting or insensitive, you will shut the other writer down. Here are some comments that can help writers develop a draft:

<@> :-) **HELPFUL COMMENTS** -O :-> ;-<

1. Have you thought about _____?
2. I don't understand this.
3. Could you add an illustration or example here?
4. Could your introduction include a stronger attention getter such as _____?
5. Could your conclusion suggest some particular resolution to the problem?
6. This is what I understood from your draft (in a sentence or two). Is this what you want to say?

:-> :-) **Try This** :-O ;-)

Help Other Writers Improve Their Essays　Read three messages in the class list and write responses. Try to be as specific as possible. Comments such as "Good job, Sonja" aren't very helpful. On the other hand, personal attacks and name calling aren't helpful either. Perhaps the writer has not had some of the experiences you have had.

WRITING FOR PRINT VS. WRITING ONLINE

To be a successful online writer, you should become sensitive to the differences between writing for print or paper and writing for the screen. Often, it's more difficult to read texts on the screen than on paper. Part of this difficulty is due to the display itself and screen glare. But it's also easy to lose a sense of the whole document, since readers can see only one screenful at a time. In fact, some readers print everything out. But as readers and writers get more accustomed to the screen, fewer readers will print out messages.

In the past, writing for print or paper—letters, stories, essays, and so forth—meant writing in a *linear* manner. Since most readers of paper texts read from beginning to end and from left to right (in our culture), writers could assume that readers would keep turning pages till they came to the end of a manuscript. At any time, readers could get a sense of the whole: they knew at a glance how far they were from the beginning and the end of a manuscript. If they wanted to refer back to an earlier point, they simply turned pages until they discovered the passage in question.

But, when you write for online readers—e-mail, for example, or pages for the World Wide Web—you cannot assume that readers will start at the beginning and go to the "end." With e-mail, they may scroll through quickly and return to the beginning of the message to respond. With the Web they may jump into your hypertext at an unpredictable pont and never see the whole of the document. When you write for the screen, think in terms of chunks of information. Connect your chunks by posting an outline at the beginning of your message. Put the most important information at the beginning of your document rather than using a leisurely introduction to entice your reader. Be direct, be concise, and be clear.

:-> :-) **Try This** :-O ;-)

Turn an Argument Essay into a Persuasive E-mail Message   How are the two pieces of writing alike? How are they different? What are the advantages of one type of writing over the other? What are the disadvantages? What kind of writing do you think will be the most common in the future? Why? Share your discoveries with your classmates, either online or face-to-face.

JOINING A SPECIALIZED LISTSERV

After you have participated in the class list, you will be ready to launch into the wider world of online discussions. There are thousands of different discussion lists on the Net—each one specializing in a different area of interest.

To find some lists of interest to you, first do some exploring in your head: Make a list of topics of interest to you. Then do some online searching to find listservs on the topics of your choice. (See instructions in Finding Lists to Join). You may have to try several terms before you find the right one. For example, if you are interested in whales, you may not find a list if you search so specifically. If frustrated in your search, try a more general term such as *environment.*

Note: In addition to finding lists on Listserv, you can also search on Listproc or Majordomo. Most academic lists are found by searching Listserv.

FINDING LISTS TO JOIN

Send e-mail to listserv@listserv.net. Leave the subject line blank. In the message field, write *list global/* and the topic you are interested in. For example, you might write *list global/environment* to see if any listservs are dedicated to discussing the future of the environment.

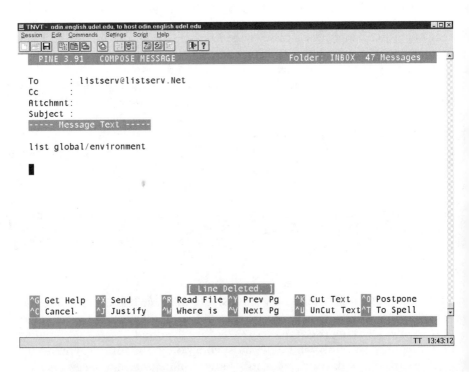

If you try this command, you will get a list of more than 100 groups you could subscribe to. Be selective: some of these groups talk about the physical environment of earth, sea, and sky; others talk about virtual environments, or classroom environments. Before subscribing, read the descriptions carefully.

To see a sample of the hundred groups found by searching under *environment,* go to the end of this chapter.

DANGER: INFORMATION OVERLOAD

f you write to listserv@listserv.net, you may get a very long file, depending on your topic. The list can clog your computer's file server or overload your directory. To avoid information overload, send specific search terms instead of general terms.

Subscribing   Once you find a list that looks interesting, it's easy to subscribe. Just send e-mail back to listserv@listserv.net, following the directions on the screen, and your message will be forwarded to the list.

You can also write directly to the list itself, using this format: listserv@ host.domain (fill in the address for your own list in the spaces called *host* and *domain*). For example, if you are interested in the future of the manatee as an endangered species, you might decide to subscribe to DIALOG-AGUA-L, a list based at the Florida Center for Environmental Studies. If so, you would write to the list address: DIALOG-AGUA-L@CENTAURI.CES.FAU.EDU (note the uppercase letters). Leave the subject line blank. In the body of the message write: *subscribe DIALOG-AGUA-L your first name and your last name.* Then send the message the way you usually send e-mail (in Pine, Ctrl-X). If you have successfully subscribed, you should receive a welcome message. Save that message in a file called Lists, so that when you want to unsubscribe at the end of the semester or when you want to find out who else is a member of the list, you will have the FAQ (frequently asked questions) file on hand.

:-> :-) **Try This** :-O ;-)

Search for a List to Join and Send a Message to Subscribe   If you first attempt fails, try again. If you get "error" messages, read them closely. Often problems in subscribing to lists come from errors in the address of the listserv. Check the address and try again. After you have subscribed, you may want to "lurk" for a while to get a feel for the culture of the list before joining the discussion.

WORLD WIDE WEB INFORMATION ABOUT LISTSERVS

f you know how to locate pages on the World Wide Web (see Chapter 5), go to *http://tile.net/listserv/* to find descriptions and information about many listservs.

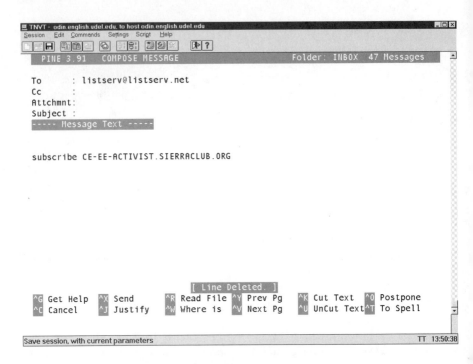

"Lurking"   When you first join a list, it's a good idea to "lurk"—to refrain from writing to the list, sitting sit back and reading the messages others write. Just as it takes a while to get to know the people in your dorm or in your class, so too, it takes a while to understand how a list operates.

While you lurk, pay attention to the *culture* of the list. Notice the written and unwritten rules of Netiquette as applied to this particular list. For example, note whether the discussion is formal or informal. Whether there are "stars" who dominate the discussion, or whether the list really is a democratic forum open to all. Often you can tell after a day or two just what the "spoken" or unspoken rules of the list are. For example, how do the members of the list respond when someone asks a question? Do they tease the writer for being a "newbie"? Or do they ignore the question? Do they try to answer the newcomer and welcome him or her into the discussion? Do students seem welcome on the list, or is the list clearly too specialized or too "expert" for novices? Lurk on a few lists until you find the crowd that feels comfortable for you.

Analyzing the List   While you are lurking, save some of the messages and examine them closely. Look at the *language*. Is it filled with insider talk? Is it academic and businesslike or colloquial, street-corner talk? Is it filled with slang or jargon that only insiders understand?

Also notice who is sending the most messages: Do some people send many messages each day, cluttering up the mailbox of everyone else on the list? Or is the discussion pretty well distributed among several people? Do both men and women participate in the discussion? Does anyone seem to be silenced by the group? Are some people's comments treated with more respect than other people's comments? Are the "regulars" already involved in a lengthy insider discussion when you first log on? If so, does the discussion continue long past other people's attempts to change the subject?

Who are the people on this list? Are they professionals or amateurs with the subject(s) under discussion? Does it matter for your purposes? How have the authors shaped their messages to reach this audience? What kind(s) of purpose(s) do the authors seem to have? Use evidence from the texts to back up your assumptions.

:-> :-) Try This :-O ;-)

Write a Review of the List   What seems to be the list's purpose? Who are its participants? Would you recommend this list to other students? Why or why not? Use evidence from the text to support your opinions.

Critiquing Individual Messages: Style, Audience, and Purpose   Because of the public nature of discussion on listservs, it is important to evaluate messages carefully. Whenever you read a message, consider the authority of the writer. Who is this person? What kinds of claims is he or she making? What is the basis for the claims?

:-> :-) Try This :-O ;-)

Store Some Messages from a Listserv in an E-mail File   When you have accumulated six or eight messages, examine each one closely. Who seems to be the "authority" in this discussion? How can you tell? Does this person claim authority because of personality type or because he or she actually knows more than the others on the list? Does this person dominate the discussion because of the sheer number of posts or because of the length of the posts? Does he or she have more expertise or experience with the subject under discussion? Write a summary of the discussion and identify each time the center of authority shifts by marking changes of subject or language that indicates control.

Introducing Yourself   As a student, you should think a bit about the way you want to introduce yourself to the list. For example, if members of the list think that you want them to do your homework or your research for you, they are likely to become angry. They will either ignore your request or treat you with some hostility. But if you ask them an interesting, genuine question worthy of thought, they are likely to respond positively. If it is clear that you respect their opinions and that you are genuinely interested in your topic—not just going through busywork assigned by your teacher—you are likely to receive many useful suggestions for source material and suggestions for your thought.

:-> :-) **Try This** :-O ;-)

Examine These Two Messages   Each of these messages is an attempt by a student to join a specialized listserv, become part of the discussion, and get some information for a research paper. Which of the messages is likely to get a favorable reception by the members of the list? After you have examined these messages, write your own introduction to a specialized listserv where you have been lurking. Keep a record of the responses to your message. How do people respond to your introduction?

MESSAGE 1

Hello. I am a student in a first-year English class at the University of CommonCare, and I need some information for a paper I am writing about the care of elderly people all over the United States. Please write to me about the care of the elderly in your state or local community. Thanks.

MESSAGE 2

The discussion about assisted-living facilities versus in-home care for elderly people has been very interesting. Question: What seems to be the break-even point? At what point is it no longer practically feasible or financially prudent for elderly people to attempt to live at home? Is there a formula to determine how to make this decision? Or is the decision made on a case-by-case basis?

< @ > :-) :-(: **HATE MAIL** -(;-O :-> :-<

When you join broad-based discussions on the Internet, you may receive hateful or spiteful mail in response to one of your postings. If so, forward the mail to your instructor.

Never give anyone your postal address or telephone number!

While online correspondents may seem friendly, keep in mind that they are strangers.

Adopting a Persona   It's fun to adopt an online persona. In real life you may be judged by your appearance, your age, your sex, or your ethnicity; but online, you are judged by your *words*. Do you want to be considered witty, carefree, and casual? If so, play with puns, use emoticons (see pp. 30–31), and use slang or colloquialisms. Do you want to be considered sophisticated and erudite? If so, try using formal language with pronouns such as "one" and latinate words of many syllables.

:-> :-) **Try This** :-O ;-)

Imitate a Writer's Style   Examine some e-mail messages you have stored and try imitating the style. Look at the authority figure in the group. How does he or she achieve authority? By using technical language and references to his or her achievements? If so, write such a message to yourself or to a friend. When you feel you have perfected this tone, try sending to a list and keep track of the responses you receive. Do people begin to respond differently to your posts when you adopt a new persona?

PARTICIPATING IN COMMUNITY DISCUSSIONS

Many people find access to a community of caring online. On Sunday, January 12, 1997, Abigail Van Buren's column (Dear Abby) in the Sunday *Wilmington News Journal* featured a letter that praised the Internet, and specifically the newsgroups and mailing lists and chat areas, where people can "ask for and receive information, share experiences, and access worldwide resources on virtually any topic."

The letter writer (Lesa Farmer of Kansas City, Kansas) wrote to respond to those who criticize the Internet as a place filled with crazy people (kooks) who spew hatred and invective into cyberspace. Ms. Farmer certainly found her voice on the Internet!

> Dear Abby: It seems that everyone is aware that there is a dark side to the Internet, but I would like to let you know about another side of it.
>
> There are many ongoing charity projects on the Internet, like the Linus Project and the ABC Quilts, which provide quilts for children with AIDS.
>
> After the Oklahoma City bombing and again after the recent California fires, the chat rooms and newsgroups were full of people offering various kinds of help. Quilts were made honoring the children who died in Oklahoma, and supplies were shipped to Californians who lost their homes.
>
> A man called Magic Mike, who has access to scraps from a fabric factory, sends these scraps to quilters across the county who craft for charities, for the price of the postage. He is not only reducing the

size of landfills (where the scraps would otherwise go), but he is also providing low-cost supplies to charities that need them.

There are whole communities of people on the Internet who have never met face-to-face or spoken on the telephone, but are ready, willing and able to act whenever a call for help is transmitted.

The Internet has more caring people than it has the bad seeds we read about in the paper. It's time to turn the spotlight away from the few who are giving it a bad name and shine it on those who are quietly making this a better world through their use of the Information Age tool.

:-> :-) **Try This** :-O ;-)

Search for a Listserv for Your Favorite Charity and Join in the Discussion Discover the kinds of help people offer to the cause. Are the members of the list just sharing anecdotes or are they actually helping those afflicted with some disease or catastrophe? If you wish, contribute a message or two to the discussion. Notice the effects on you. Do you become more actively involved with this charity as a result of your participation in the listserv? Do you join in any activities or events that you have never done before? Keep an online journal about your experience with the charitable listserv.

GATHERING RESEARCH MATERIALS FROM LISTS

Some lists specialize in posting items such as news stories and documents from organizations or legislative bodies. These lists will be especially fruitful as sources for research. If you are doing a research paper, search for a list that specializes in posting information (see instructions for finding lists on p. 48).

:-> :-) **Try This** :-O ;-)

Join a Research-Oriented List Join a research-oriented list and keep a file of information obtained from that list. Evaluate the information carefully: is it accurate, reliable, complete, up-to-date? Check the name of the author or the sponsoring institution or organization. See if you can find more information about the author. Check the online source against material available in print.

When you use the information in your paper, cite sources correctly. Keep careful records of author, title, date, and address of the online source. See the Appendix for proper format on citing online sources.

Cutting and Pasting from Online Sources into Your Document Sometimes you might want to include a clip from an online card catalogue—perhaps you are sending a suggested reference to a friend. Other times, you might want to clip messages from an e-mail discussion and include them in an essay. In any case, if you are using Windows 95 or Mac System 7 or any other graphical user interface, (GUI), it's easy to cut and paste, or, rather, to copy and paste. Use the mouse to highlight the information you wish to copy, then toggle over to your other document. Choose the Edit menu and choose Paste, or use a shortcut such as command C and command V on a Mac. You may have do some careful proofreading and editing. Sometimes when you copy e-mail, for example, lines are repeated. So use cut and paste to strengthen your document by providing concrete illustrations and examples and useful information for your readers, but carefully read the final version before sending. For a polished appearance, clean up the messy edges of the cut and paste job by eliminating repetition and providing transitions where needed.

:-> :-) Try This :-O ;-)

Copy from E-mail to Your Word Processor   Open an e-mail file and use the mouse to highlight some text from a message. Go to the Edit menu and choose Copy. Then open your word-processing program to a new blank document (or to a document you are already writing). Move the cursor to the place where you want to add text. Go to the Edit menu and choose Paste. The text from your e-mail document should now appear in your word processor document. **Note:** You can also cut and paste from your word processor's documents into e-mail.

Noticing the History of a Message   When you read e-mail, notice how many times the message has been sent back and forth among various people. Look at the *greater-than* (>) signs at the left margin. Each time a new "speaker" joins the discussion, the computer program adds a > sign before each line of the old messages. For example, sometimes you may see as many as five or six greater-than signs—>>>—at a particular part of the message. You can also *check the dates and times* posted at the start of each response. To keep the history of a message straight, usually you will want to make sure that you are responding to the latest posting. But sometimes you might want to join a discussion and comment on an earlier part of the message. If so, you should make it clear in your message that you know you are responding to an earlier posting.

:-> :-) Try This :-O ;-)

Trace the History of an E-mail Message   Look at your stored e-mail messages. Find one that has several greater-than signs. Trace the history of that message. Who was the first writer? Who was the second? Was the message a simple dialogue between two writers, or did others participate, too? Write the history of a message.

Special Options   Sometimes you will want to give instructions to the listserv to hold mail while you are on break or to condense it in a digest. To control the flow of mail, learn to use the Nomail, Mail, Digest, and Index commands.

:-> :-) **Try This** :-O ;-)

Stop Your Mail   To send a message to your list to stop mail, send e-mail to listserv@host.domain. Keep the subject line blank. In the body of the message write *set listname (fill in the name of your list) nomail.* Then send the message. To resume normal delivery, send another message that says *set listname mail.*

Create a Digest   Send a message to your list to create a digest to hold all the mail for twenty-four hours and send it all as one big message. To do this, send a message to the listserv. In the body of the message write *set listname digest.* To change back to the normal way of receiving mail, send another message to the listserv that says *set listname nodigest.*

The Index commands tells the listserv to send a single message every day that describes all the notes distributed by the list during the day. If you use this command, you can then ask for delivery of notes only on the particular topic that you are interested in. To try this, send the listserv a message that says *set listname index.* To begin receiving mail normally, send another message that says *set listname noindex.*

Archives   If you have limited space on your e-mail account, you might not want to save lots of messages in your own files. Since most public lists are "archived," you can delete messages from your own files and still find them online by visiting the computer where the list resides. For example, if you have subscribed to a list that is sent from the University of Arkansas, for example the list for art students, you could send a message to listserv@uafsysb.uark.edu asking if the list is archived. You would leave the subject line blank, and in the body of the message write *index artist-l.* If no archive is kept, the listserv will send a note saying that the index file is unknown. If an archive is kept, the listserv tells you how long the files are kept and whether they are kept weekly or in some other format. You can then request a copy of the files by using the Get command. For example, you would write *get artist-l log9701,* and you would get a copy of the log for the month of January 1997.

:-> :-) **Try This** :-O ;-)

Discover if the Files Are Kept in an Archive   Send a message to the listserv for one of the discussion lists you belong to asking if the files are archived. If the listserv says *yes,* use the Get command to get a copy of the archives for a specific period. Before deleting messages stored in one of your own files, always check to see if there is an archive of the list.

COMMON PROBLEMS

Joining a listserv is usually informative and fun, but sometimes you may get frustrated with common problems. Following is a list of problems and how to solve them:

1. *Errors in addresses or commands.* Often problems are caused by typing the wrong character—especially by confusing upper- and lowercase letters such as the numeral one (1) and the letter *L* (l). If you get an error message, see if you have typed the address or command properly.
2. *Sending a message to the wrong person.* Sometimes writers send messages to the people on the list when they should be sent to Listserv or Listproc. For example, if you want to sign off of a list for the summer or at the end of a semester, you should send the signoff message to the software—not to the discussion (see instructions for unsubscribing below).
3. *Using the right commands for the wrong program.* Sometimes you may be on a mailing list run by Listserv software; other times you may be using Listproc or Majordomo. If you keep getting error messages, send a one-word command to the software: *help.* You should then get a list of instructions on how to do the things you are trying to do.
4. *Not being recognized by the computer.* If you subscribe from one address and then send a command from another address, the software may not be able to identify you. If you get frustrated, send a message to the list owner—a human being! To find out the address of a Listserv list owner, send e-mail to listserv@host.domain (fill in the address for your list). In the message write *review listname short.* You will receive a message identifying the owner of the list. There are similar commands for Listproc and Majordomo.

Unsubscribing   When you are ready to leave the list, send a message to the listserv@host.domain. In the body of the message write *signoff* and the name of the list: for example, *signoff food-1.* Remember to leave the subject line blank.

:-> :-) **Try This** :-O ;-)

Why Are Listservs Popular? Now that you have had some experience with listservs, read the following paragraph by Nancy Matthews on "The Real Reasons for Listservs." Do you agree or disagree with Ms. Matthews about the reasons for the popularity of lists? Write a response to this paragraph in an e-mail message and share it with your classmates. Why do *you* think listservs are gaining popularity every day?

< @ > **"THE REAL REASONS FOR LISTSERVS"** :-<

By Nancy Matthews

Why are listservs becoming increasingly abundant on the Internet? Because millions of people find common links with other online personalities whose interests and concerns parallel their own. Discussion groups allow everyone with access to the Net to voice opinions about subjects with no censorship limitations, with a certain degree of anonymity, and with other people willing to listen. Listservs serve as a form of escape from the formalities necessary in traditional public writing, allowing users to express their truest feelings and receive some sort of response. Listservs serve many functions, but primarily they compensate for loneliness in a mobile society. They also serve as a source of entertainment and information, linking people separated by vast geographical spaces into a community of common concerns.

SAMPLE LISTSERV DISCUSSION

Here are some listservs you might want to join.

LISTS THAT DISCUSS THE ENVIRONMENT

Be careful. There are many meanings for the word *environment*. Note that addresses are all caps. Be sure to use the caps key when you type the addresses.

Date: Sat, 13 Sep 1997 18:23:22 +0200

From: "L-Soft list server at SEARN (1.8c)"
    <LISTSERV@SEARN.SUNET.SE>

To: mhalio@udel.edu

Subject: File: "LISTSERV LISTS"

Excerpt from the LISTSERV lists known to LISTSERV@SEARN.SUNET.SE

13 Sep 1997 18:23
(search string: ENVIRONMENT)
Copyright 1997 L-Soft international, Inc.
L-Soft international, Inc. owns the copyright to this compilation of Internet mailing lists (the "Compilation") and hereby grants you the right to copy the enclosed information for the sole purpose of identifying, locating, and subscribing to mailing lists of interest. Any other usages of the Compilation, including, without limitation, solicitation, tele-marketing, "spamming", "mail-bombing" and "spoofing" are prohibited.

```
*************************************************************
* To subscribe, send mail to LISTSERV@LISTSERV.NET with the *
* following command in the text (not the subject) of your   *
* message:                                                  *
*                                                           *
*      SUBSCRIBE listname                                   *
*                                                           *
* Replace 'listname' with the name in the first column of the *
* table.                                                    *
*************************************************************
```

Network-wide ID Full address and list description

AERE-LAERE-L@LSV.UKY.EDU
Association of Environmental and Resource Economists

ANNOUNCE ANNOUNCE@ITSSRV1.UCSF.EDU

ANNOUNCE ANNOUNCE@ITSSRV1.UCSF.EDU
Changes to AdCom computing environment

BECCNET BECCNET@LISTSERV.ARIZONA.EDU
Border Environment Cooperation Comm & N. Amer. Dev. Bank

CAMASE-L CAMASE-L@NIC.SURFNET.NL
Quantitative Methods of Research on Agricultural Systems and

+

CAMPUSCARE-L CAMPUSCARE-L@POSTOFFICE.CSO.UIUC.EDU
campus environments for children

CDE-L CDE-L@LISTSERV.SYR.EDU
Common DeskTop Environment

CDROMLANCDROMLAN@IDBSU.IDBSU.EDU
CDROMLAN—USE OF CDROM PRODUCTS IN LAN ENVIRONMENTS

CDROMLANCDROMLAN@IDBSU.IDBSU.EDU
CDROMLAN - USE OF CDROM PRODUCTS IN LAN ENVIRONMENTS

CE-EE-ACTIVISTS CE-EE-ACTIVISTS@LISTS.SIERRACLUB.ORG
Sierra Club Environmental Education Activists List

CERES-L CERES-L@WVNVM.WVNET.EDU
Collaborative Environments for Conserving Earth Resources

COASTALP COASTALP@URIACC.URI.EDU
URI Partnership for the Coastal Environment Bulletin Board

COCE-L COCE-L@YORKU.CA
Environmental Communication List

CST-L CST-L@YORKU.CA
Learning and Teaching in the University Environment list

CUSEN-L CUSEN-L@QUCDN.QUEENSU.CA

CUSEN-L CUSEN-L@QUCDN.QUEENSU.CA
Canadian Unified Student Environmental Network

DIALOG-AGUA-L DIALOG-AGUA-L@CENTAURI.CES.FAU.EDU
The Florida Center for Environmental Studies Dialog-Agua-L

Mai+

DLO-E-INFO DLO-E-IN@NIC.SURFNET.NL
Info on Dutch research on agriculture, nature, and environment

ECDM ECDM@PDOMAIN.UWINDSOR.CA
Environmentally Conscious Design & Mfg List

ECO-FUND ECO-FUND@UMDD.BITNET
Discussion Of Environmental Finance Issues

EEN-L EEN-L@PEACH.EASE.LSOFT.COM
Discussion list for evangelicals and the environment.

EEN-L EEN-L@PEACH.EASE.LSOFT.COM
Discussion list for evangelicals and the environment.

EFIEA EFIEA@NIC.SURFNET.NL
Bulletin Board European Forum on Integrated Environmental

Asse+

EHOS-MAIL EHOS-MAIL@HOME.EASE.LSOFT.COM
The Environmental Health Officers' International Mailing List

EHS-L EHS-L@LISTSERV.OKSTATE.EDU
Environmental, health and fire safety issues on campuses

EHS-L@UGA.CC.UGA.EDU
Environmental Health Sci. Club

ENTREE-L ENTREE-L@NIC.SURFNET.NL
Environmental Training in Engineering Education

ENV-TALK ENV-TALK@LIST.UVM.EDU
Environmental Program Discussion List

ENVALUM ENVALUM@LIST.UVM.EDU
UVM Environmental Studies Alumni/ae Network

ENVINF-L ENVINF-L@NIC.SURFNET.NL
List for Environmental Information

ENVIRON ENVIRON@MIAMIU.ACS.MUOHIO.EDU
Miami University Environmental Information

ENVIRONMENT_C . . . ENVIRONMENT_CONFLICT_MEDIATION-L@
    CLEMSON.EDU
ENVIRONMENT CONFLICT MEDIATION

ENVIRO98 ENVIRO98@LISTSERV.UOGUELPH.CA
Environmental Science 98

ENVIRO99 ENVIRO99@LISTSERV.UOGUELPH.CA
Environmental Science 99

ENVISAT-L ENVISAT@NIC.SURFNET.NL
About the European Environment Satellite ENVISAT and its

senso+

ENVJOBS ENVJOBS@HERMES.CIRC.GWU.EDU

Environmental Jobs / Internships

ENVSCI ENVSCI@LIST.UVM.EDU
Environmental Sciences in the College of Arts & Sciences

ENVSMETHODS ENVSMETHODS@LIST.UVM.EDU
Environmental Studies Research Methods

ENVST-L ENVST-L@BROWNVM.BROWN.EDU
Environmental Studies Discussion List

ENVST-L@LISTSERV.VT.EDU
Listserv for Environmental Studies at Virginia Tech

ESE-L ESE-L@CCVM.SUNYSB.EDU
Expert Systems Environment mailing list.

ESTAS2 ESTAS2@LIST.UVM.EDU
Environmental studies 2

EXT-ENV-BUS EXT-ENV-BUS@LISTSERV.UIC.EDU
External Environment of Business

FID-NEIS FID-NEIS@NIC.SURFNET.NL
FID NEIS - NATIONAL ENVIRONMENTAL INFORMATION SYSTEMS

DISCUSSI+

FIELDING_ENVIRONMENTAL_SOLUTIONS@AEC2.APGEA.ARMY.MIL
FIELDING ENVIRONMENTAL SOLUTIONS LIST

GREENGRP GREENGRP@HERMES.CIRC.GWU.EDU
Inst. for the Environment

H-ASEH H-ASEH@H-NET.MSU.EDU
American Society for Environmental History (H-NET List)

HEALTHE HEALTHE@HOME.EASE.LSOFT.COM
Health and Environment Resource Center

IFEJLIST IFEJLIST@MSU.EDU
Int. Fed. of Environmental Journalists

ISEA-L ISEA-L@NIC.SURFNET.NL
International Students for Environmental Action

ISEA-L ISEA-L@NIC.SURFNET.NL
International Students for Environmental Action

KEREM KEREM@JTSA.EDU
Jewish Theological Seminary environmental network dedicated

to+

KOL-CHAI KOL-CHAI@JTSA.EDU
The COEJL list for Jewish environmental action and discussion

LAB-XL LAB-XL@LIST.UVM.EDU
Environmental Regulation of Laboratories

LIVEGREEN LIVEGREEN@LIST.UVM.EDU
Environmental Ethics for Daily Living

MAX MAX@VM1.MCGILL.CA
Discussion of interactive music/multimedia standard

environmen+

MUD-L MUD-L@VM3090.EGE.EDU.TR
Multi-User Dungeons and Other Simulated Real-Time Environments

NATOSCI NATOSCI@CC1.KULEUVEN.AC.BE
Information on the NATO Science and Environment Programmes

OHPETE-L OHPETE-L@LISTSERV.KENT.EDU
Ohio PETE Environmental Education Information Exchange

OPSENV OPSENV@IRISHVMA.BITNET
Operations Work Environment Team

PS248 PS248@UMSLVMA.UMSL.EDU
PS248-ENVIRONMENTAL POLITICS

PV-HSE PV-HSE@NIC.SURFNET.NL
Health, Safety, and Environmental Aspects of Photovoltaic

Techn+

QEN-L QEN-L@POST.QUEENSU.CA
Queen's Environmental Network

QUEST QUEST@LISTSERV.NODAK.EDU
Quality, Environment, Safety in Management

RIVERTEAM RIVERTEAM@HOME.EASE.LSOFT.COM
RIVERTEAM: Environmental action in northeast Florida

SBENVS-L SBENVS-L@UCSBVM.UCSB.EDU
"UCSB Environmental Studies List"

SC_ENVIRONMEN . . . SC_ENVIRONMENTAL_EDUCATION-
L@CLEMSON.EDU
SC ENVIRONMENTAL EDUCATION

SCAN-L SCAN-L@VM.OCC.CC.MI.US
Oakland Community College Environmental Scanning Issues

SEAUGA SEAUGA@UGA.CC.UGA.EDU
Students for Environmental Awareness Univ. of Georgia

SENSE-L SENSE-L@AMERICAN.EDU
Environmental club

SSC-WAR SSC-WAR@NETSPACE.ORG
Sierra Student Coalition War on the Environment

TERRAMON TERRAMON@MORGAN.UCS.MUN.CA
TerraMon - Long-term environmental monitoring in Nfld. & Lab.

TF-ETINU ETINU@GUMNCC.TERENA.NL
TERENA Task Force on Environment To Inspire Network Users

(TF-+

TREE TREE@LISTSERV.VT.EDU
TREE Taking Responsibility for the Earth and the Environment

TW-ENV TW-ENV@LISTSERV.SYR.EDU
Taiwan Environment

UNITE-L UNITE-L@VM1.HQADMIN.DOE.GOV
DOE UNified Information Technology Environment

UNT-GREENUNT-GREEN@UNT.EDU
Green Environmental Organization

VEIL VEIL@UGA.CC.UGA.EDU
Virtual Environments Interactive List

WIOLE-L WIOLE-L@MIZZOU1.BITNET
Writing Intensive Online Learning Environments

15–345F97-L 15–345F97-L@LISTSERV.UOGUELPH.CA
Intro to Aquatic Environments

15–34568-L 15–34568-L@LISTSERV.UOGUELPH.CA
Intro. to Aquatic Environments

C H A P T E R

T H R E E

USENET NEWS GROUPS: FRONTIERLAND

USENET NEWS GROUPS DEFINED

Usenet groups are online "places" where people interested in a particular topic gather to "talk." They differ from listservs because the messages in a newsgroup do not come directly to your mailbox; instead, you must subscribe to the group and use a "reader" such as Netscape Navigator or TRN to read the discussion and to post responses. There are thousands of newsgroups on line and millions of participants. The groups provide a forum for anyone interested in expressing an opinion on any subject. Often compared to ham radio or to radio talk shows—the voice line of the people—they are usually much less academic than listservs. There are newsgroups online from prisons, from hospitals, from organizations such as Alcoholics Anonymous, from community centers, from parents' organizations, from fan clubs for movie stars and rock stars, and even from nursing homes and day-care centers—any place people gather.

In fact, the idea for this book started because of an experience two of my students had with a Usenet group. Darrell and Sharon, both minority students, joined a newsgroup on the subject of race, and both were deeply affected by the experience. Because of the hate speech he found there, Darrell became so angry that he turned inward and refused to write to the discussion. On the other hand, Sharon, after an initial period of self-imposed silence, decided that she was not going to let these hateful voices muzzle her. She rejoined the discussion and began to answer the hate with reasoned opinions. Sharon challenged writers to defend their points with evidence and specific illustrations and examples. As she wrote, her online voice became strong, and her offline essays took on new power. More importantly, *she* changed, too. She gained confidence in her newfound ability to express her ideas and to challenge the voices of hate and unreason.

You, too, can use participation in newsgroups to find a stronger voice.

USING A READER

To participate in Usenet groups, you will need to use a "reader." Readers are software programs that provide an interface for reading, composing, posting, and downloading newsgroup messages. You may use commercial software such as Windows Explorer or Netscape Navigator or free software downloaded from the World Wide Web such as Free Agent News to read newsgroups. When you load the software, use the instructions provided by the documentation to set up or "configure" the options you want. For example, if you are using Netscape, click on the Options menu and choose Mail and News Preferences. Then, from the Servers option, check the settings for News. Select the location where you want to store news: if you use Netscape from your own PC, you should specify C: drive as your storage space for newsgroups. But if you use Netscape from a mail server, you should specify your home directory: for example, */home/hostname/yourusername*. Next, select Identity and enter your e-mail address and your name as you want it to appear on outgoing messages. Finally, click OK and close the Preferences dialogue box. You are now set up to read newsgroups.

:-> :-) **Try This** :-O ;-)

Set Up Your Options   Load the software you wish to use for reading news. Using the instructions provided in the documentation, set up the options the way you prefer. When you have finished setting the options, go on to Finding a Newsgroup to Join.

FINDING A NEWSGROUP TO JOIN

There are many ways to find newsgroups. Sometimes you will see a list of interesting-sounding groups in magazine articles or in books such as this. (See a list of popular newsgroups at the end of this chapter.) Other times, you can use your news reader to search online for groups.

If you want to search the WWW for groups, point your browser to http://www.dejanews.com to do a keyword search on a topic of interest. DejaNews is helpful two ways: (1) you can search for messages on the topic of your choice and it will display messages from many newsgroups, or (2) you can search for the groups that are likely to be talking about your topic. You can also try http://www.jazzie.com/ii/internet/newsgroups.html; http://www. infoseek.com; and http://www.search.com.

:-> :-) **Try This** :-O ;-)

Search for Groups to Join   Use your newsreader to search for groups to join or point your WWW browser such as Netscape or Internet Explorer to the dejanews site or the nova site at http://www.nova.edu/Inter-Links/cgi-bin/ news-lists.pl. If you don't have access to the WWW, or if you are uncertain how to navigate the Web, you can still subscribe to newsgroups using software such as TRN on a mainframe computer. To subscribe using TRN, see the documentation for this software. If you are uncertain how to access the Web, see Chapter 4.

WARNING: PUBLIC SITES AND NETSCAPE OR EUDORA OR EXPLORER

eading mail or newsgroups using Navigator, Explorer, or Eudora at a public site (not on your own PC) can cause problems. For example, when you set the Options preference to tell the newsreader where you want messages sent, you cannot usually specify another computer or terminal; therefore, your messages will continue to go to the public terminal site until someone else changes the settings. This could be a confusing or embarrassing experience (depending on which groups you subscribe to).

If you must read newsgroups or mail at a public site, it is best to use your mainframe or UNIX account if possible. If you read newsgroups using UNIX, the software will probably be TRN or TIN.

SUBSCRIBING TO A NEWSGROUP

Once you have found a group you would enjoy belonging to, you can "subscribe" by choosing to add that group to your reader. For example, if you are using Navigator on a PC, go to the File menu and choose Add Newsgroup. If you are using a Mac, go to the Window menu and open Netscape News. Type the name of your group. It will then appear in the list of groups on the screen whenever you read newsgroups. To make sure that the group will be in your list the next time you choose to read news, click on the box next to the name of the group.

:-> :-) **Try This** :-O ;-)

Join a Newsgroup   Open your newsreader and go to the option to add a group. Type the name of the group (if you don't have a group to join, use the WWW to search dejanews.com or see the list below). When the group's name appears on your subscription list, click on the box next to the name (if you are using Netscape). Then, as the messages arrive in your box, click on the group's name and read the messages.

If you don't have access to the Web to search for groups, here are some groups you might join:

misc.fitnessFAQ

alt.yoga

rec.food.restaurants

sci.ed.nursing

talk.politics.medicine

alt.folklore.urban

alt.folklore.herbs

alt.recovery.addiction

If you have a particular interest or hobby, chances are there is a group named *alt.yourhobby* (fill in the name of your hobby) or *rec.yourhobby.* Try typing the name you imagine (for example, *alt.guitar* or *rec.skating*) and see what you find.

Reading a Newsgroup Once you have selected a newsgroup to join, spend some time reading the messages before posting. Just as it's a good idea to wait a while before entering a conversation at a party so you can see who's saying what, so too it's a good idea to lurk for a while and "listen" carefully to the discussion. To get a feel for the flow of ideas and to see who dominates the discussion, read some of the messages. Notice the addresses of the participants. For example, one of my students once subscribed to a newsgroup on prison literacy programs. It took a while before she realized that some of the messages were coming from prisoners in maximum security prisons! As she "lurked," she began to see that the richest posts were coming from some of the prisoners—not the so-called criminal justice experts. Her point of view about prisons and who lives there began to expand.

:-> :-) **Try This** :-O ;-)

Monitor the Group As you lurk, make some notes about the kinds of messages you see posted and get a feel for the discussion. In your online journal, write a one-paragraph description of the discussion in this group. Post your description to the class listserv and tell your classmates whether you recommend this group or not and why. Use examples from the discussion to support your opinion.

Critical Thinking When reading messages in newsgroups, it's important to evaluate the posts critically. Some posts may make you angry; others may bore you or make you sad. To participate fully in newsgroups, you should get in the habit of stepping back a bit from the messages and asking yourself, "What am I responding to here?" Is it the language, the tone, or the content? What has made you angry, bored, or sad?

Also, it's important to think about the validity and reliability of the information found in newsgroups. Remind yourself often to think about the evidence presented. Who are these people? Sometimes you should go to print sources to check out the information on the newsgroups. Other times, you can check the credentials of a writer by visiting his or her WWW page or by looking up his or her professional qualifications (see Chapter 4). *Get into the habit of questioning* everything *you read—both online and offline— and you will be well on the way to reading critically and interactively.*

:-> :-) **Try This** :-O ;-)

Analyze the Membership of One of the Newsgroups   Who *are* these people? What is their level of expertise in the subject under discussion? Do they know the subject by reading and researching or by life experiences? For example, if you have joined a group on single parents or divorce, try to decide which participants know firsthand about the trauma of divorce and which have only studied it in books. Keep a list of participants and write a profile of each one.

POSTING MESSAGES AND RESPONSES

After you have lurked for a while, you will probably feel ready to reply to someone else's message. It's very easy to do that. Using Netscape, and many other readers, just click on a Reply icon or press R to reply. You may also want to *start a new thread of discussion*—particularly if you think the current thread is going nowhere. New readers are sometimes shy about starting new threads, but this is a chance for you to find a real audience and purpose and to practice stating your ideas concisely and powerfully, so go ahead and post a new thread!

Caution: Nuts on the Net   When you join a newsgroup, do not divulge your home address or phone number in a message or in a signature file. Remember that these messages are very public and can be read by millions of people!

As in any new crowd, it's important to protect your identity. Writers may seem extremely friendly, but notice that very few messages indicate the location of the writer precisely. Just like the veteran posters, you, too, should *protect your privacy and safety* by guarding your address and phone number. If you choose to identify yourself later in a one-to-one e-mail discussion, use discretion.

:-> :-) **Try This** :-O ;-)

Respond to a Newsgroup Message   In one of the newsgroups you are monitoring, choose one of the messages that interests you or puzzles you and plan a response.

A good response will challenge the writer to explain his or her opinion or to substantiate unwarranted or unsupported claims. A good response will help the original writer to clarify his or her thinking.

After you have experimented with posting responses to others' messages, *try starting a new thread* by posting a message of your own that will take the discussion in a new direction. Just as in an offline conversation, a good new thread will raise a subject that is interesting to the readers of the newsgroup and broad enough to invite many different opinions. Often a question that asks for opinions on a topic of interest to the group will start a new thread. Try it!

Notice whether your post prompts a new discussion. If not, try again. Keep a record of your attempts to change the thread. Analyze your attempts and report your experience to your class list.

<@> :-) (KEEPING RECORDS ;-O :-> :-<

Get into the habit of keeping records—online in a file folder or offline in a notebook—of who said what, when, and where. For example, if you are reading a newsgroup dedicated to the discussion of health care, you might record that on July 18, 1998, iamaphysician@medico.com in the newsgroup talk.politics.medicine said that "the government should not interfere in the patient–physician relationship."

Later, you might use that quote in a paper comparing the attitudes of health-care professionals and the general public on the subject of government subsidy. If you have kept careful records, you won't be wondering where you got that quote.

VALUES AND STANDARDS

Often people post messages without examining their own prejudices and assumptions. *Underneath our values and standards, each of us has certain assumptions.* For example, if I believe that capital punishment is wrong, it's probably because I believe in the value of every human life—even the life of a murderer. Or it may be because I believe that all human systems are flawed; therefore, humans make mistakes; therefore, the criminal justice system is imperfect; therefore, capital punishment should not be carried out because the system may have unjustly convicted an innocent person. To convince me that my stand on capital punishment is wrong, someone would have to examine my assumptions and figure out a strategy of counterargument.

:-> :-) **T r y   T h i s** :-O ;-)

Identify Underlying Assumptions   Examine the postings of an individual you disagree with in one of the newsgroups you monitor. If this individual takes a strong stand on an issue such as censorship on the Internet (pro or con), for example, try to reconstruct why this person might feel the way he or she does. What are his or her values and standards? If she argues that freedom of speech is guaranteed by the First Amendment to the Constitution, you can probably assume that she thinks the Constitution is the first law of the land and that law is a social good that protects the freedom of the individual for the good of all. If, on the other hand, he argues that the Net should be censored because children use it, you may be able to assume that the writer is in favor of the control of the spread of ideas because some people in the society must be "protected" by those who know better. To critically analyze the opinions of others, you must be aware of their reasons for believing as they do. Then you can begin to articulate your own beliefs and why yours might differ from theirs. After you have analyzed the postings of someone you disagree with, frame a response, challenging them to defend their assumptions.

NEWSFEEDS

Some newsgroups post information from news sources such as the Associated Press. These groups are often identified as Clari or Clarinet newsgroups. Since these groups can be useful sources of information for research papers, check with your librarian or system administrator to see if they are available at your school. You can also identify these groups if you search online and find groups that start with *clari.* For example:

> clari.biz.* . . .
>
> clari.feature.* . . .
>
> clari.local.* . . .
>
> clari.nb.* . . .
>
> clari.net.talk (discussion of Clarinet-only unmoderated group)
>
> clari.news.* . . .
>
> clari.sfbay.* . . .
>
> clari.sports.* . . .
>
> clari.tw.* . . .
>
> clari.world.* . . .

The Clari newsfeeds can be a wonderful source of information for history papers or for the discussion of any current events.

When I searched AltaVista for Clari, I got the following list of "hits." This is a list of ten "documents matching the query." According to the screen display, there were about twenty thousand matches!

Search and Display the Results

Tip: Do not use AND or OR to combine words, simply type a few words or phrases.

Word count: clari:132678

Documents 1–10 of about 20000 matching the query, best matches first.

Clari-Net NewsNote: You must be a subscriber to P-Net in order to receive the news listings below. Internet Hourly News. News around the clock, at 15 minutes past the . . .

http://www.mo.net/info/clari.html—size 33K—19 Apr 96

Newsgroup list:clari.*

Newsgroup list:clari.* ClariNews enables you to get today's news faster than any newspaper can bring it to you, and in more depth than any newspaper can . . .

http://www.interport.net/interport/news/news_clari.html—size 14K—30 Nov 96

ClariNet e.News via the Web: clari.living

Living. Living. Animals. Arts. Bizarre. Books. Celebrities. Consumer. Entertainment. Good News.

History. History Today. Human Interest. Movies. Music. . . .

http://www.visi.net/news/living.html—size 3K—1 Dec 96

ClariNet e.News via the Web: clari.nb

VisiNet News: NewsBytes. Apple. Macintosh products, Apple Corp. Broadcast. Interactive television, cable TV. Business. Business and industry news. Chips . . .

http://www.visi.net/news/newsbyte.html—size 4K—1 Dec 96Newsgroups available under clari

Newsgroups available under clari. Back to top level. clari.biz.* . . . clari. feature.* . . . clari.local.* . . .

clari.nb.* . . . clari.net.talk Discussion of . . .

http://c38.npt.nuwc.navy.mil/Library/NewsGroups/Server1/clari.html—size 876 bytes—13 Feb 95

Newsgroups available under clari.biz

Newsgroups available under clari.biz. Back to top level. clari.biz.economy.* . . . clari.biz.features Business

feature stories. (Moderated) . . .

http://c38.npt.nuwc.navy.mil/Library/NewsGroups/Server1/clari.biz.html—
size 1K—13 Feb 95

Newsgroups available under clari.feature
Newsgroups available under clari.feature. Back to top level. clari.feature.dil-
bert The daily comic strip
"Dilbert" (MIME/uuencoded GIF). (Moderated) . . .
http://c38.npt.nuwc.navy.mil/Library/NewsGroups/Server1/clari.feature.html
—size 539 bytes—13 Feb 95

Newsgroups available under clari.local
Newsgroups available under clari.local. Back to top level. clari.local.arizona
Local news. (Moderated) clari.local.california Local news. (Moderated) . . .
http://c38.npt.nuwc.navy.mil/Library/NewsGroups/Server1/clari.local.html—
size 3K—13 Feb 95

Newsgroups available under clari.nb
Newsgroups available under clari.nb. Back to top level. clari.nb.apple Newsbytes Apple/Macintosh news. (Moderated) clari.nb.business Newsbytes business &..
http://c38.npt.nuwc.navy.mil/Library/NewsGroups/Server1/clari.nb.html—
size 1K—13 Feb 95

Newsgroups available under clari.news.labor
Newsgroups available under clari.news.labor. Back to top level.
clari.news.labor Unions, strikes.
(Moderated) clari.news.labor.strike Strikes. (Moderated).
http://c38.npt.nuwc.navy.mil/Library/NewsGroups/Server1/clari.news.labor.
html—size 457 bytes—13 Feb 95

MODERATED GROUPS

The messages on these groups have been filtered through a moderator;
therefore, hate and rants are generally removed. When you join a newsgroup, check to see if it is *moderated* or *unmoderated*. Sometimes this information appears in a brief description of the group or in a FAQ file
available online. If in doubt, ask.

News.announce.newusers: The First Stop   A good example of a moderated
group is *news.announce.newusers*. This group posts information of importance to people new to newsgroups. It covers writing style on the Net, Netiquette, and working with the "community" of users. This group is
moderated by experts.

If you are using Netscape, you can find this group by pulling down the Windows menu and choosing Netscape News. Since new users are automatically subscribed to news.announce.newusers, you should see the name of this group in a list at the left side of the screen when you log on. If you click on the name, you will see a message of vital information on reading newsgroups. *You are requested* not *to post to this group.* Instead, send e-mail to mail-server@rtfm.mit.edu requesting copies of the documents described in the *news.announce.newusers* group.

You should also see another group called *news.newusers.questions.* It's fine to post to this group. In fact, this is where most people post their first message. Many subject lines say *test, don't read.* People just want to see if they can post a message. You will also see questions about finding newsgroups to join or about access to newsgroups from non-English-speaking people. Many languages are represented in this newsgroup. This is a good place to hang out until you feel comfortable with groups.

:-> :-) **Try This** :-O ;-)

Read the FAQs for Newsgroups   Load your newsreader software (Netscape Navigator, Internet Explorer, Trumpet News, TRN, etc.) and find the group called news.announce.newusers. Select this group and read the messages. Remember, don't post messages here. Then select news.newusers.questions and post a message to the group. If you are using Netscape, you can post a message by clicking on the Post or Reply icons at the top of the screen. When you reply to a message, you can choose to reply in the public space, or to send "private" e-mail to the writer (remember that e-mail is never really private). If you are using software other than Netscape, follow the instructions in the documentation for posting.

UNMODERATED GROUPS

Unmoderated groups have no filter; therefore, *every message sent to the list will be seen by everyone.* Some messages may be scholarly and precise; others may be hate-filled rant or imprecise information. There are often long "threads" of discussion on a particular issue. You can usually identify the threads by the subject line. Use your delete key to dump the threads you are not interested in. Unmoderated groups offer the liveliest discussion, but you should read with great care and lurk for a while before posting. You just might get "flamed"!

Groups that begin with the prefix *alt, rec,* or *talk* are unmoderated. Here you will encounter all kinds of people and all kinds of opinions. In a real sense, this is the frontier of the Internet. Danger lurks, but so do discovery and excitement.

:-> :-) **T r y   T h i s** :-O ;-)

Search DejaNews   If you know how to access the World Wide Web (see Chapter 5), search dejanews.com to find a group on a topic of your choice and subscribe for a week or two. Keep a record of the posts in this group. To save messages, cut and paste them into your word processor, or send them as e-mail to yourself.

After you have gathered the messages, classify the posts into categories of your choice. For example, which posts would you classify as academic or substantiated? Which posts are opinions from life experience? Which posts seem meant to provoke an argument? Which posts seem genuine? Which seem fabricated or false? To substantiate your opinions about the post, refer to the language or the content.

After classifying the posts, write an analysis of the group, in a formal essay or as a creative piece of writing in which you bring the online people to life, describing what you think they look like or act like. *Show, don't tell,* why certain writers seem attractive to you and others do not.

If you interested in exploring other kinds of controversy on the Internet, join some newsgroups where people talk about homosexuality.

:-> :-) **T r y   T h i s** :-O ;-)

Lurk in a Controversial Group   Join two or more of the following groups and analyze the discussion. Which group(s) seem to be serious discussions about the problems faced by homosexuals in modern society and which seem to be places for people to post hate messages? Do any of the groups serve any other function(s)? *To substantiate your opinion, save posts and use them as data or illustrations and examples.*

alt.politics.homosexuality

bit.listserv.catholic

alt.atheism

alt.homosexual

bit.listserv.gaynet

rec.arts.startrek.current

seattle.politics

rec.org.mensa

alt.christnet

can.politics

seattle.general

alt.fan.rosieodonnell

alt.showbiz.gossip

Following are groups where people talk about African Americans. Subscribe to two or more of these groups and lurk for a while. Which groups are serious discussions of the problems/opportunities faced by this minority group? Which are hate groups? Use evidence from the text to support your opinion.

soc.culture.african.american

alt.fan.oj-simpson

alt.california

alt.politics.nationalism.white

talk.abortion

FINDING A COMMUNITY

In real life, all of us belong to several communities—our family, our friends, our classmates, our college, our neighborhoods, and specialized communities such as social clubs or campus organizations or special interest groups such as people trying to save the environment. Online, we can find many different virtual communities—across the city, or across the world; we can have access to friends and information we would not be likely to find on our block or in our residence hall or apartment building. To see how Heather Newman found a new community on the Internet, read the following essay.

"NET NEWSGROUPS OFFER WORLD OF INFORMATION"

By Heather Newman

When you're a geek and the icemaker in your fridge quits working, there's only one place to go: the Internet. And that's just were I went when, after months of flinging tiny cubes across the freezer compartment, my icemaker got bored and refused to even take in water.

If you're expecting me to tell you about some great refrigerator repair page on the World Wide Web, think again. No, I went straight to that collection of opinionated homeowners and appliance repair nuts (professional and otherwise) that hang out on alt.home.repair.

In less than 24 hours, I had a pile of responses, including several from professional appliance mechanics. We pinpointed the problem as the solenoid that controls the release of water into the ice tray, a fairly easy part to replace.

Bingo. Got my answer and didn't pay $45 an hour to someone who needs a tighter belt. But what is this *alt.home.repair* place, you ask?

Tucked away on the millions of computers that make up the world's largest computer network are discussion groups dealing with nearly every topic under the sun: 15,000 of them, ranging from people who love people named Courtney to fans of ceiling fans to my friends at alt.home.repair.

They're called Newsgroups, and nearly everyone with access to the Internet (including CompuServe or America Online users) can scroll through them.

If e-mail is like an electronic postal service, Newsgroups work like a community bulletin board; I wander over and post a message. You walk by and see it. Maybe you post a reply. Maybe you send me mail about what you read. Or perhaps you choose to post a message on some other topic altogether.

To see Newsgroups, you need a news reader. There's a reader built into Netscape Navigator and Microsoft Explorer.

But like most free add-ons, the news readers built into these programs are lacking for any but the most casual users. There are plenty of stand-alone news readers available for downloading off the Internet. My current program is Trumpet News Reader, a simple program that, like most, lets you view ongoing threads or topics of discussion, post replies, or send mail, and search for groups you want to join.

The nice part of all news readers is that they keep track of what you've read. It's sort of like being able to take down all the message off the bulletin board once you've scanned them: the only notes you see when you walk by are ones that have been posted since the last time you visited.

Not sure what groups to visit? DejaNews, at http://www.dejanews.com, lets you search for Newsgroups messages that contain the words or phrases you type in.

Those messages will identify what Newsgroups they were originally posted in (like misc.consumers.frugal-living or alt.barney.dinosaur.die.die.die) a good clue to which groups you might like.

Trumpet News Reader is available for download at http://www.trumpet.com.au. If you're running Windows 95, Anawave's Gravity news reader is excellent and can be found online at http://www.microplanet.com. Apple users can find links to a couple of readers at http://222.mcp.com/hayden/iskm/iskm-soft-table.html.

Now if someone can just direct me to a cheap source for solenoid valves.

Source: *The Wilmington News-Journal,* Monday, Oct. 28, 1996, p. D7. Copyrighted by *The Tennessean (Nashville).*

:->   :-) **Try This** :-O ;-)

Analyze Newman's Style   Heather Newman's style is effective in this article. Who is her audience? What is her purpose? *Provide illustrations and examples from the text to support your assumptions about her audience and*

purpose. In addition to writing an amusing anecdotal piece, Newman also provides useful information about how to begin reading newsgroups. *Make a list and summarize the information provided in the article. Then check out the information.* How much of it is still useful? How much of it is out of date? (The Net moves quickly!) In a paragraph, evaluate Newman's article or write an article of your own about an online community that helped you solve a problem.

CRITIQUING A THREAD: MULTIPLE POINTS OF VIEW

When you first start reading newsgroups, you will notice that there are "threads" of messages—all with the same subject header. An easy way to get acquainted with a group is to follow a thread. See who's saying what. See which threads produce some interesting conclusions and which seem to lead nowhere.

:-> :-) **Try This** :-O ;-)

Join a Newsgroup and Follow a Thread   Read all the messages that have the same subject header (using Netscape, you can sort messages by subject). Analyze the discussion. Does this thread have lots of "knots" in it that tangle up the ideas? Or does it weave itself into a coherent whole? Save the messages on a specific thread and report on this discussion in an e-mail to the class list. Based on your analysis of this thread, would you recommend this newsgroup to your classmates? Why or why not?

If you don't have access to the World Wide Web, or if you are uncertain how to use it, there is a list of suggested newsgroups to try at the end of this chapter.

WHAT'S IN A NAME?: ALT.GOO OR COMP.GOO?

When you scan the Web or a printed list of Usenet groups, you may, at first, feel bewildered by the names. For example, what's the difference between *alt.politics.irish* and *comp.politics.irish*?

In general, groups that begin with the prefix *alt* tend to be informal; with the prefix *comp,* formal and serious. Others are *rec,* recreational; *news,* sometimes formal, sometimes informal; *sci,* serious science; and *misc,* general information.

Short Cut Sometimes you may want to scan some groups to find out where your topic is being discussed. Using the resources of the company Reference.Com, you can enter a search term and scan twenty-two thousand indexed newsgroups and mailing lists to find out which ones are talking about your topic. Then you can have the results e-mailed to you directly or saved for you at Reference.Com's "clipping service." To try Reference.Com, go to its Web site, http://www.reference.com. If you are uncertain how to access the site, see Chapter 5.

Recently a student searched Reference.Com for information on alcoholism. Although Maria was particularly interested in students' problems with alcohol, her first search was under the general term *alcohol.* It yielded 4,582 "hits": lists of messages, newsgroups, and authors.

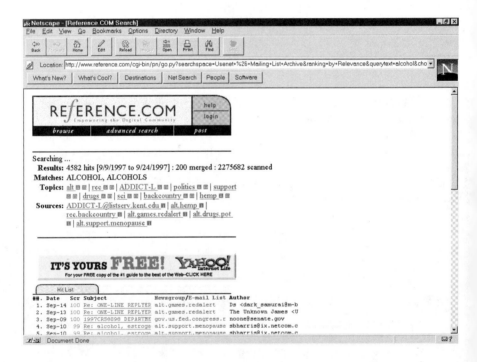

Maria found that several newsgroups are listed as Top Sources for discussions about alcoholics: alt.recovery.aa; alt.recovery.addiction.sexual; alt.recovery.codependency; alt.abuse.recovery; and alt.obituaries. She also found a listserv dedicated to the subject of alcoholism: ADDICT-L@listserv@kent.edu. But she felt that her search was too broad. She decided to narrow her focus and search for *students and alcohol.* This time the search yielded 379 hits.

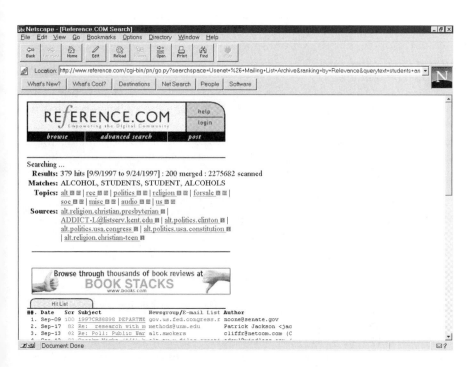

She scanned the first twenty-five hits of this search and realized that she wanted to focus her search even more. Next, she searched under *students and alcohol and recovery.* This search yielded only twenty-three hits—a manageable number.

Finally, Maria decided to join a newsgroup (alt.recovery.addiction) and a listserv (ADDICT-L@listserv.kent.edu). By lurking for a while and then participating in the discussion, Maria was able to get some anecdotal evidence and insight into students' problems with alcohol addiction. Using the insights gained from her online community, she developed a survey that she administered to students in her residence hall. She also visited the wellness program at her university and talked to the counselors there about the student Alcoholics Anonymous group on campus. Because of her online research, Maria was able to bring a vitality to her paper that it would have been difficult for her to obtain from print materials.

:-) :-) **Try This** :-O ;-)

Join a Newsgroup Related to a Major Health or Social Problem   Join a newsgroup related to a major health or social problem on your campus— drug or alcohol addiction, eating disorders, sexually transmitted disease, or some other problem. Lurk for a while, then participate in the discussion as an interested and compassionate observer. Make notes or save messages about your participation in the newsgroup. *Then, using the insights you have gained, develop a questionnaire for students on your campus on the topic you have investigated.* Finally, compare the situation on your campus to the insights you gained in the online discussion. Is the situation on your campus similar to or different from the online community? To validate your observations, you may wish to consult some print sources in the library or electronic databases (see Chapter 4) using keywords developed from your topic.

The debate about the censorship of hate groups online continues to rage. Here is one student's opinion. Do you agree with David? If so, why? If not, why not?

< @ > "BIGOTS ON THE NET: FREE TO SPEAK?" :-<

By David Persoleo

D iscussion groups or Usenet groups can be used by anyone to present their views to a wide audience—even hate groups. Almost everyone with computer access has entrance to the Internet and to the Usenet groups that can be found there; therefore, many more people than in the past can read the message of hate. Since our communication is tainted by hate mail, we must be aware of it and try to stop its spread. But how? Should the Internet be censored by the companies that allow access to it?

Private companies have banned white supremacists who were causing trouble in a news group. Also, some groups devoted entirely to hate were taken down by the access providers. But the Net should *not* be regulated for adults; it should be regulated only in terms of age because children are unformed and impressionable. Teachers or parents can tell the children about the groups and then explain why they are wrong.

It is *not* fitting for hate groups to be denied access to the Web. If I have something to say, then I should be able to say it. *The same applies to bigots.* We are in this country together, and we cannot restrict the free expression of ideas because of what people think. If we cannot stop people from thinking the way they do, then how we expect them to keep quiet? Morally their ideas may be repugnant, but freedom of speech is what sets us apart from the rest of the world. Let's keep it that way!

:-> :-) **Try This** :-O ;-)

Explore Censorship of Usenet Groups
Write an entry in your online journal exploring your opinion about censorship of Usenet groups. Then subscribe to one or more controversial groups such as bigots or political radicals. Keep a record of the dialogue in that group. Then write an analysis. Compare your impression after participating in one of the groups to your preparticipation opinion. Have you changed your mind as a result of your experience online? (See the instructions for Finding Usenet Groups on p. 67).

Controversy of Another Kind: Revisionists and the Holocaust
Recently, when I clicked on ClariNet e.News via the Web: clari.living, I found a site that lists several newsgroups that talk about history. One group in particular (*alt.revisionism*) talks about the Holocaust that happened during World War II in the Nazi death camps in Europe. Although the death of six million Jews, Gypsies, Poles, and others in the camps is a well-documented historical fact, some people argue that it never happened. This newsgroup is a moderated list maintained by the Nizkor Project: An Electronic Holocaust Education Resource Southwestern Research Center at http.//www.nizkor.org to provide a forum for debunking those who would call the Holocaust a hoax.

:-> :-) **Try This** :-O ;-)

Analyze Hate Messages
If you wish to subscribe to alt.revisionism, see instructions on Subscribing to a Newsgroup, p. 68. **Warning:** Angry, hostile messages are posted to this group. The language is often offensive and even frightening. If you do decide to lurk in the group, I suggest you *analyze the discussion in some depth before even considering posting.* Notice who is name calling and who is supplying evidence and data. Notice who is trying to spread anti-Semitic hate with remarks about Jews in powerful places in government and banking. Write a report about this group in your online journal,

using posts from the group to substantiate your position. Who *are* these people? Why do they spend many hours on the Internet discussing the Holocaust?

Warning: Be especially careful to protect your identity in this group or in any group that discusses minorities such as gays, lesbians, or Mexican Americans. Participation in groups of this type can be an excellent experience in learning how to spot the language of hate, but it's important to be aware that some groups attract radicals and extremists of every stripe.

WHO'S ONLINE?

Internet newsgroups are filled with "experts" and ordinary folks and everyone in between. If you join a newsgroup on a topic you are researching for a paper, you may have a chance to ask a question of the leading people in the field. This is particularly true if your topic deals with a current issue such as health care or physician-assisted suicide. But experts are busy people. *If you want to ask a question, you should do your homework first.* Your question should show that you have thought through an issue. For example, if you join a discussion on physician-assisted suicide, you shouldn't just ask if it is right or wrong. That question is far too broad. Instead, you might ask if there is any case where it is clearly wrong for a physician to assist a patient with committing suicide. Then, the online experts and others can offer a concrete example.

:-> :-) Try This :-O ;-)

Join a Newsgroup and Lurk   You might choose a group on a social or health problem, or you might be interested in joining a group on a sport or a hobby, for example: rec.martial-arts, misc.fitness.misc, misc.fitness.aerobic, misc.fitness.weights, rec.arts.dance, alt.arts.ballet, or rec.sport.misc. While you lurk, see if you can discover any online experts on your topic. You will probably be able to identify these experts either because their names are well known or because they are able to answer others questions thoughtfully and precisely with detailed data or evidence.

When you have determined who the experts are, frame a question to get their opinion. For example, recently I joined a newsgroup on yoga. I lurked for a while, then realized that there were yoga teachers in the crowd and people who had written books about yoga. Finally, I asked if anyone could recommend a form of yoga that would give me a good cardiovascular workout as well as strengthening my muscles and increasing flexibility. Several experts replied; some to the whole group, others privately to me through e-mail. By "talking" to experts online, I was able to get the answer I needed (Kundalini yoga provides cardiovascular benefit as well as the traditional benefits of stress reduction and increased flexibility). I also enjoyed "talking" with the experts, who turned out to be kind, thoughtful people.

WHO ISN'T?

It's important to remember that, although millions of people are on the Internet, billions are not. According to several popular sources, the average Internet user is a thirty-five-year-old white male American with an annual income of approximately fifty-thousand dollars. Although the numbers of women and minorities on the Net are growing exponentially, there is still a considerable gap. Also, the overwhelming number of Internet users speak, read, and write English as their first language; therefore, most of the texts online are in English. But English is not the only major language in the world, nor should it be. Millions of people in third-world countries are not represented on the Internet because their countries do not have the technological infrastructure—the cables, mainframe computers, and so forth—needed to support the Net; therefore, their opinions are often missing in debates about population control or the ecology or global pollution. Sometimes people in less affluent parts of the world connect to the Internet via a modem, but they must pay high telephone rates and connection charges to a service provider for the privilege. Contrary to popular opinion, information on the Net is *not* free and open to all.

:-> :-) Try This :-O ;-)

Join a Human Rights Newsgroup   Join a Usenet group on a subject of concern to women, minorities, or people in the third world (for example, human rights). Analyze the membership of the group. Is the discussion dominated by young, affluent men with e-mail addresses in the corporate world or affluent schools? Or is the membership of the group diverse, international, multicultural, and democratic? Save posts from the discussion to support your opinion. If you are interested, do some research (see Chapter 4) and get more information about Internet access in a particular underdeveloped part of the world, or in a less affluent part of your own city or state. Develop a thesis arguing for or against better Net access and support in the geographical area you have researched.

FINDING YOUR PLACE

Sometimes when you join a new group, you may not be sure how to find your place. Should you represent yourself as a student and ask questions openly? Or should you try to blend in with the crowd and be an observer? Sometimes you might want to play with an identity—to adopt a persona—especially in a social group. But if you decide to research a social or health problem or to ask insiders about politics in a developing country, for example, it can be dangerous to adopt an identity that may be offensive to the group you stepped into.

  Recently, one of my students decided to join a newsgroup about eating disorders. At first, Beth spoke as a student, asking the participants facts

about their eating and probing into their family history (her thesis concerned domineering parents). Quickly, the participants turned on her. Angry
that she would use them (and their problems) as subjects for her paper, they
told her to "get lost." They resented her attitude. They felt she viewed them
as some sort of guinea pigs or rats in a maze.

Fortunately, Beth had the courage to stay in the group. She apologized
to them and told them that she had become interested in the subject because she was concerned for a friend (true story) who might have a disorder.
Immediately, the group's attitude toward Beth changed. They welcomed her
as a participant in the discussion. They asked her about her friend and
shared stories and resources. Although Beth was able to get some anecdotal
evidence from this discussion to use in her paper on eating disorders, she
did so *by permission—not by spying.* She felt good about her experience
with online newsgroup research, and I suspect the participants in the group
felt better for having educated her about how to talk with people with a
health problem. The experience was valuable for Beth. It changed her attitude. She matured considerably and grew as a researcher because of her experience talking with people with problems.

:-> :-) **Try This** :-O ;-)

Learn About a Health Problem by Participating in a Newsgroup   If you are
interested in researching a health problem such as alcohol or drug addiction
or eating disorders, search for a newsgroup or two on the subject. Lurk for a
while in the group. Then carefully pose some questions. *Do not misrepresent yourself to the group.* For example, do not claim to be addicted yourself,
but show an openness to learn from the experience of others.

Getting "Lost" in Cyberspace   Because of the seductive nature of the Usenet,
it's easy to lose yourself in the mass of messages. When people talk about
their perceived need for censorship of the Net, they often refer, for example,
to the morass of pornographic or bigoted or hateful discussions online.
Given the fact that we can "become" a new person online, sometimes our
real self can get lost in the labyrinth. Getting lost can mean having trouble
navigating the maze of messages. That can be disorienting itself. But even
more troubling is the feeling of getting sucked into a discussion that you
would never participate in offline. Sometimes people become someone online that they would not dream of being offline.

:-> :-) **Try This** :-O ;-)

Analyze Your Online Behavior   Keep a journal of a week's time spent on the
Internet. Record as precisely as possible how much time you spent online

and what you did. At the end of the week, write a report to yourself or to your classmates about your journey through cyberspace. Where did you go? Whom did you talk to? What did you see? What voices did you hear? What voices did you *not* hear? Did you find yourself engaging in any discussions you would have avoided in the real world? If so, do you think your time was wasted or well spent? Why? Did you ignore your real-life friends and family while participating in the virtual world of the Internet?

Use the impressions you have gathered to argue for or against increased use of the Internet by young people.

Playing with Audience: Clarity and Support   Newsgroups are a good place to practice sounding professional. Often by simply adjusting your pronouns from *I* and *you* to *we* and *us,* you can begin to sound like one of the community. Also, you should aim for simple, clear prose and support your observations with evidence and illustrations.

:-> :-) **Try This** :-O ;-)

Find a New Voice   Sometimes you can use your participation in a newsgroup to experiment with a new *voice*. To test this trick, join a newsgroup related to your major (or to a field you have some interest in majoring in). Lurk for a while until you begin to feel at home with the group. Then, *imagining yourself as a prospective professional in this field, post a question or a reply to a question.* For example, if you are studying nursing, you might post a question

WRITING TO NON-ENGLISH SPEAKERS

Usenet groups will give you a wonderful opportunity to write to people with vastly different experiences of life and points of view that differ greatly from your own.

Sometimes you might write to people who are new speakers of English—especially if you are writing on the subject of immigration or bilingualism. You might also try writing to an international audience with multicultural participants on a subject such as the war in the former Yugoslavia.

If you are writing to speakers of English as a second language, keep your sentences brief and your vocabulary plain and precise. Don't use in-jokes and plays on words, for example, about some American television show or film. Be aware of the differences in culture.

regarding the treatment of postsurgical patients using the plural pronoun "we." Or if you are a business major, you might venture an opinion about some new marketing procedure or some way to finance a new undertaking. Try for a professional voice. Use "we" whenever possible to achieve a feeling of inclusion in the new community. Record your experience in the group and your feelings about joining a discussion in the profession you wish to enter.

WORLDWIDE READERS: OTHER LANGUAGES

If you read a language other than English, or if you are learning a new language, newsgroups offer the perfect place to practice structures, vocabulary, and sensitivity to a different culture. If you join such a group, you will have an opportunity to interact with people who can give you a broader picture of the world than you may already have.

:-> :-) Try This :-O ;-)

Participate in a Foreign-Language Newsgroup   Search for a newsgroup from another country (or a newsgroup from the United States in which people may write in Spanish or some other language). Often you can spot a foreign newsgroup because the name ends in the name of another country. Also, *look at the e-mail addresses of the people posting messages to the group.* If they end in an abbreviation for another country (*ca* for Canada, *it* for Italy, *uk* for United Kingdom), subscribe to the group. Lurk for a week or so, then post a message.

To practice your second-language skills, try composing your message with a word processor and cut-and-pasting it to the newsgroup. *Be aware that you should have special sensitivity to the culture of the group.* If the group writes excellent Italian, for example, check your grammar and vocabulary before posting. Also, be aware that Americans are sometimes known for having a superior attitude. You are likely to have far less knowledge of the language and culture than the other participants in the discussion, but if you prepare your messages carefully, you should gain much from the experience.

This exercise will be particularly useful if you are planning to study or travel abroad. By writing to international readers, you will get a feel for the major issues under discussion in the target culture. This exercise will also help if you are writing an essay on a subject about which you need a different perspective. For example, if you are writing about bilingual education, it would help to discuss this subject in a Spanish-speaking group.

Keep a careful record of the discussion, noting particularly points of view that differ from your own. Store interesting messages in an online file. Keep notes about the name of the newsgroup and the date. Record the name and e-mail address of the writer, so you will have this information handy if you choose to quote or summarize the discussion in your own essay.

TIPS FOR WRITING TO INTERNATIONAL READERS

To write to readers from a different culture, it is important to bear in mind that you need to think about more than correct language. You also need to think about culture. Here are a few tips:

1. *Attitudes toward time and change may differ from culture to culture.* In some cultures, speed (the quick reply) may be a virtue; in others, it may not.
2. *Attitudes toward change and "progress" may differ from culture to culture.* In some cultures, change is a positive value and newness is thought of as progress. In other cultures, change is viewed negatively; instead, tradition is valued.
3. *Attitudes toward directness and indirectness may vary from culture to culture.* In some cultures (typically Western), directness, conciseness, and clarity are highly valued in writing. In other cultures, indirectness, fullness, and ambiguity are more highly valued.

ARE NEWSGROUPS A WASTE OF TIME?

Analyze your experience with newsgroups in this chapter. What have you learned? Would you recommend that other students use newsgroups to get experience writing to real audiences for real purposes? Why or why not? Using illustrations and examples from your experiences, post an essay to your class list arguing for or against student participation in newsgroups.

NEWSGROUPS TO JOIN

Television and Violence
    rec.arts.drwho

    misc.activism.progressive

    rec.arts.startrek.misc

    misc.kids

    rec.arts.tv

    alt.censorship

Pollution and Environment
    sci.environment

    finet.freenet.kidlink.response

alt.religion.scientology

talk.environment

sci.energy

uk.environment

AIDS

misc.health.aids

sci.med.aids

sci.med

misc.health.alternative

alt.homosexual

gay-net.aids

Pregnancy

misc.kids.pregnancy

alt.infertility

Dating and Relationships

soc.singles

soc.culture.asian.american

alt.romance

news.newusers.questions

soc.culture.african.american

soc.couples.intercultural

alt.polyamory

sdnet.singles

alt.support divorce

Smoking and Health

alt.smokers

alt.support.stop-smoking

alt.smoker.cigars

bionet.sci-resources

sci.med

College and Money

rec.games.trading-cards.marketplace

rec.arts.tv.soaps.abc

soc.college.financial-aid

news.groups

misc.invest.funds

alt.child-support

misc.invest.stocks

comp.infosystems.www.authoring.html

alt.college.us

soc.college admissions

soc.college

misc.education

Parents

alt.adoption

misc.kids

alt.wedding

alt.tv.highlander

bit.listserv.autism

alt.parenting.solutions.

alt.christnet

alt.tv.seinfeld

bit.listserv.deaf-l

bit.listserv.down-syn

k12chat.teacher

alt.support.single-parents

alt.gothic

rec.humor

misc.kids.pregnancy

Parents and Teenagers
misc.kids

alt.adoption

alt.parenting.spanking

alt.christnet

alt.parents-teens

talk.abortion

misc.kids.info

Parents and Child Abuse
misc.kids

alt.parenting.spanking

alt.adoption

alt.activism

alt.child-support

alt.abuse.recovery

Capital Punishment
alt.activism.death-penalty

bit.listserv.catholic

nz.general

aus.politics

talk.politics

uk.politics

alt.atheism.moderated

Stock Market
> misc.invest.stocks
>
> misc.invest
>
> misc.invest.technical
>
> misc.invest.funds
>
> misc.invest.canada
>
> misc.invest.futures
>
> alt.business.misc
>
> misc.entrepreneurs

Crime and Prevention
> talk.politics.guns
>
> alt.activism.death-penalty
>
> misc.activism.progressive
>
> alt.law-enforcement
>
> bit.listserv.politics
>
> can.talk.guns
>
> misc.legal
>
> alt.crime
>
> talk.rape

Crime and Punishment
> alt.activism.death-penalty
>
> uk.politics
>
> misc.kids
>
> alt.fan.dragons
>
> talk.rape
>
> alt.prisons
>
> alt.law-enforcement

FINDING SOURCES ONLINE: MINING THE TREASURE TROVE

The research process is daunting—especially on the Internet. Since there are thousands of possible sources online for any given topic, writers are faced not only with enormous possibilities but also with incredible challenges. How do you dig through the tons of rock to find the rich veins of ore? How do you separate the ounces of gold from the tons of dross?

But if you find a treasure, the search is well worth it. And like the '49ers in the California Gold Rush, you may have a few adventures along the way. For example, you might start out on your research journey with a quest for information on *toxic waste* and wind up investigating a local scandal about government corruption regarding the disposal of waste. Along the road, you may find some facts, figures, and people who will surprise you and even alarm you—all while sitting at your computer keyboard.

The Internet research journey is not for the faint of heart. It can be time consuming and exhausting, but the finds can be astounding. There is information online from remote libraries, community organizations, businesses, research organizations, the U.S. government, environmental agencies, professional organizations, commercial enterprises, educators, medicine, news and current events, social science, women's studies, race, social class, gender, religion, and recreation. Much of this information is not available anywhere else. Especially if your topic is timely, you will probably find the most up-to-date and complete information online. Print sources always lag behind the Internet—especially since developments occur at an astounding rate in many fields such as technology.

Even if your topic is an historical event about which much has appeared in print, you should still check the Internet for recent information. For example, you might be doing a paper about the Civil War; if you check the Net, you might find recently discovered information about the weapons used, or new information about diseases or medical treatments that affected the course of the war, or DNA information about some famous person who was influential in the war. So if you want to be a careful and knowledgeable researcher, in addition to checking sources in conventional libraries, you should learn how to mine the Internet.

How do you deal with information overload? Because the Internet has thousands of talk groups and millions of home pages, it's easy to get lost in the maze. To be an effective Internet researcher, you must have a *search strategy*. That means you must spend some time before getting online thinking about your topic and narrowing and focusing. Do some prewriting, brainstorming, list making, or clustering. Develop some questions you want to investigate—debatable issues about which there is (or may be) disagreement among the experts. Then you are ready to launch your quest.

SHIFTING SANDS

Because sources on the Internet frequently change addresses (uniform resource locators, or URLs) and information, sometimes you will be digging in quicksand.

Some sources, such as Web pages, are works in progress. Writers "construct" sites, adding new wings, raising the roof, and framing in windows. Because these home pages are built on a fluid foundation, they are exciting and stimulating, but they are also somewhat treacherous. Other online sources, such as archived e-mail lists, documents available by file transfer protocol (FTP) or Gopher, may change, too. Authors can post an updated version of an essay with new data and new findings.

So, where should you dig? Look for relatively stable sources such as those found on university sites or at major publications such as the *New York Times*. An address containing a ~ (tilde), for example, http://www.udel.edu/~harry, means the person who wrote the page is affiliated with an institution, but that person might leave.

To avoid problems with sinking sites, keep careful records including time and date of the dig and save the source on a diskette or in a printout. That way you'll have the record of your dig and you can share it with other "miners" if you wish.

Here is one student's description of her research paper process. Allyson describes her trek through traditional sources and notes several advantages of doing research on the Net. She also addresses problems students face putting all the information together and using sources to support an argument.

< @ >   : "MY RESEARCH PAPER PROCESS" - >   : - <

By Allyson B.

I really don't like to do research papers. I find them to be hard and very annoying. I found this paper to be especially frustrating. I was nervous going to the library and not knowing where everything was located or how to find any sources. When I did finally get up the nerve to go, I went there with my E-110 Student Guide to the Library and tried my hardest. But when I did this I spent two hours there only to find that either the books were not in or they weren't what I was looking for. *This made me angry!*

I found the Internet easier because at the library all the books are thick and you aren't sure if they contain what you are looking for, while on the Internet you just skim right through and look for keywords that pertain to your topic. Also, because no one takes the sources "out" on the Internet, they are there waiting for you. The Internet is quick and easy. I found some Usenet groups on my subject (eating disorders). I also found several articles and a listserv. *I recommend it for students.*

Another source that I am using is an *interview.* This can be a good way to understand what real people think on your topic. I found the information that I gathered through interviews to be the best in my paper. *It is very direct and really gave truth to my paper.*

I am having problems putting my paper together. I feel as if I have so much data and nowhere to put it all. I tried making an outline but found that I have leftover information and it doesn't fit into the paper. To me this material seemed to be vital to my paper, but I guess this isn't true.

I have taken a few of my ideas for my paper around to others to look over. *The girls in my hall have proved to be good peer editors.* They are frequently reading over my work to see if I made any errors or if there is room for improvement. When I am completed with the rough draft of my paper I plan on taking it over to the Writing Center for the same reasons I let my friends help, but this time by professionals.

Overall, I am not finding the research paper to be difficult but rather a pain. It takes a lot of time and effort. *Next time I will not put it off as long as I did and maybe then it won't be such a bother.*

Allyson did an excellent job of describing her research paper process. Is her experience similar to yours? If you have written research papers in the past, have you experienced frustrations?

: - >   : -) **T r y   T h i s** : -O ;-)

Describe Your Research Paper Process   Write a paragraph or more describing your past experience with doing research and putting it together to write a paper. Which parts of your research and writing were easy? Which were difficult? What do you think you would like to change about your process? *Post your thoughts on the class listserv and compare your experience to the experience of others.*

RESEARCH PAPERS VS. REPORTS

As you work on your research, it is important to keep in mind that you need to write an *essay*—not a report. What's the difference? A report is simply an accumulation of facts, figures, statistics, and anecdotal evidence. It is an All-You-Ever-Wanted-to-Know-About-____ sort of thing. But a research paper, unlike a report, has a *thesis*. It takes a point of view. *A research paper sticks its neck out and takes a position on a subject.*

As you do your research, look for a *debatable topic*—one on which there are conflicting opinions. Then examine the evidence pro and con. *Look for sources on both sides of the question.*

Finally, when you are ready to write your paper, take a stand. Create a thesis (see a sample paper on p. 123) and support your thesis with evidence from your research.

The Research Process: Narrowing and Focusing Before you start looking online (or in your campus library), you should narrow and focus your topic as much as possible.

It's pointless to search the Net (or your library) for a broad subject area such as the Vietnam War. You will receive far too much information, much of it general and all of it distracting from the research process. You might want to read some general information, probably available from your library, as background about the war. But when you launch onto the Internet, you should have a particular focus about the war.

For example, you might want to investigate "draft dodgers" or protest marches, or the Vietnam War Memorial and its design, or a particular battle, or protest groups, or songs or movies about the war (compare and contrast), or the role of women in the war (American or Vietnamese), or the treatment of Vietnam veterans both at the end of the war and currently in America.

The point is, if you want to find useful information on the Net, *you must plan a strategy*—make a road map—before setting out on your journey, or you will not make it to the gold.

GOPHER, FTP, AND THE WORLD WIDE WEB

Increasingly, researchers use the WWW to retrieve information from the Internet, but it's still a good idea to know the basics of the older information retrieval systems such as FTP (file transfer protocol), WAIS (wide-area information server), Fetch (Macintosh), and Rapid Filer (Windows) that have been used to transfer documents from a distant computer to your own computer. Basic information is provided in this chapter on p. ***. For details, check with your campus computing center or with your instructor.

Long before the WWW was created, Gopher (software developed at the University of Minnesota and named for the university's mascot) was used to search the Internet for files by using keywords. Gopher can still be used if you do not yet have access to the Web. It provides a list of menus that you can step through layer by layer to find vast quantities of information. Unlike the Web, Gopher provides text only (no sound or graphics). Basic information on using Gopher is provided in this chapter on pp. 100–104. For details, check your campus computing center.

:-> :-) **Try This** :-O ;-)

Create a Search Strategy for a Topic of Your Choice   You can begin either online by looking at a search engine such as Yahoo! that uses a subject-tree directory, or offline by doing some prewriting, list making, brainstorming, or clustering.

For example, Jessica, the student who was interested in writing about the Vietnam War, first did some free writing on the subject. She wrote random thoughts—everything she knew about the war:

- things her parents had told her
- things she had seen on television
- things she had read in history class
- movies she had seen.

When she finished her free writing, she looked back over the page and circled ideas that looked interesting to her. She realized that Vietnam issues seemed to be filled with both fact and myth. She noticed that somehow the Vietnam War had made Americans mistrust the government. She wondered why this had happened.

Jessica decided to focus on the question of the treatment of veterans after the war. Were the movies accurate? Had veterans really been called "baby killers" and murderers? Did they really step off of the plane into hostile or apathetic crowds? Instead of having victory parades such as those that happened after World War II, were people spitting on vets or harassing them? If veterans were mistreated and the government did nothing to stop the mistreatment, is this why the government seemed untrustworthy?

Jessica knew that she had no answers, but she also knew she had some interesting, debatable questions.

She decided to begin her online search by using the university's online public access catalog (OPAC), an electronic card catalog. She wanted to curl up with some books and page through some magazines to get a feel for the period of history. Jessica logged on to the computer in her residence hall room and found that several sources were available at her school's library. She recorded the *call numbers* for these books and magazines, walked to the library, and spent an afternoon browsing. She brought some materials back to her room for a second look.

Next, Jessica decided to investigate other libraries. She knew that if she found books and articles elsewhere by using her school's Gopher system, she could go to Interlibrary Loan and request that the source material be sent to her. She used a handout obtained from her campus computing center to find out how to use the Gopher system. Using the menu available on the Gopher screen (see printout below), she chose to Telnet to other schools and look at their OPACs. She discovered that her school's library contained most of the books she found through the Gopher, but she also found a master's thesis that was not available in her library and asked for it to be sent to her through interlibrary loan.

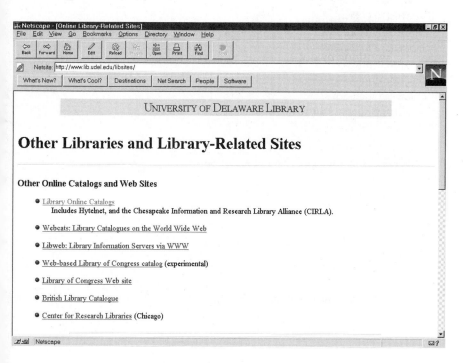

Root gopher server: gopher.uXyz.edu

—> 1. U-Discover! Xyz's Internet Gopher Server/
2. News and Weather/
3. Telephone, E-mail, V-mail, and Other Directories
4. Campus News/
5. Campus Events and Activities/
6. General University Information/
7. Library Information/
8. Computing & Technology/
9. Employee Information/
10. Student Information/
11. Uxyz Department, Program, & College Information Services/
12. Public Safety/
13. Off-Campus Information Services/
14. Search U of XYZ U-Discover! Menu Titles <?>

Internet Gopher Information Client 2.0 pl8

Library Information

1. About the Library's Web Site.
2. The URL is: http://www.lib.udel.edu.
3. DELCAT <TEL>
4. ABI/INFORM/
5. Current Contents/
6. OCLC FirstSearch <TEL>
7. CARL UnCover <TEL>
8. Course Reserves Lists/
9. Electronic Forms/
—> 10. Online Catalogs of Other Libraries/
11. Special Collections/

Internet Gopher Information Client 2.0 pl8

Online Catalogs of Other Libraries

—> 1. Catalogs of the United States/
2. Catalogs Listed by International Location/
3. Library of Congress Online Systems (LOCIS)/

Internet Gopher Information Client 2.0 pl8

Catalogs of the United States

—> 1. Alabama/
2. Arizona/
3. Arkansas/
4. California/
5. Colorado/
6. Connecticut/
7. Delaware/
8. Florida/
9. Georgia/
10. Hawaii/
11. Idaho/

ETC . . .

Jessica chose to look at catalogs at schools in Pennsylvania.

1. Allegheny College <TEL>
2. Allegheny College.
3. Bucknell University <TEL>
4. Bucknell University.
—->5. Carnegie Mellon University <TEL>
6. Carnegie Mellon University.
7. Chatham College <TEL>
8. Chatham College.
9. Clarion University of Pennsylvania <TEL>
10. Clarion University of Pennsylvania.
11. Dickinson College <TEL>
12. Dickinson College.
13. Drexel University <TEL>
14. Drexel University.
15. Edinboro University of Pennsylvania <TEL>
16. Edinboro University of Pennsylvania.
17. Franklin and Marshall College.
18. Franklin and Marshall College <TEL>

When she logged on to the system to access Carnegie Mellon, Jessica was surprised to see a warning:

Warning!!!!!, you are about to leave the Internet Gopher program and connect to another host. If you get stuck press the control key and the] key, and then type *quit*.

Connecting to gopher.lib.uXyz.edu, port 3000 using Telnet.

For the first time, she had a sense of travel on the Internet. It gave her a feeling of adventure! Suddenly the research-paper process seemed like it could be a real journey of discovery.

The next screen welcomed her to—

Carnegie Mellon University's Library Information System.
For authenticated access, please use your Andrew id and password.
For guest access, use the id "library". No password is required.
login: library
SEARCH   Library Catalog (CMU)   mercurio

Type keywords and press RETURN—or enter a command

Default is ADJ:

Welcome to LIS!
****

The location codes in the updated Catalog are different from those
in the previous version of the Catalog. The new codes are from Unicorn,
the University Libraries new library management system.
Please send questions or comments to lis-help@andrew.cmu.edu.

****

Commands RETURN: Do search OR Display list of titles in highlighted set
CTRL-N: Highlight next set CTRL-V: Show next page of sets
CTRL-P: Highlight prev set ESC V: Show prev page of sets

ESC 1: New or modify search ESC 3: Print and options ESC 5: Help on
Search
ESC 2: Change databases ESC 4: Browse index ESC 6: Quit LIS

Next Jessica chose to use the OCLC First Search and CARL UnCover to search for articles journals not found in her library. She found three articles that she needed and arranged to have them sent to her.

When she logged on to OCLC First Search, she found that she could choose to search for books or articles, or to search the table of contents of thousands of journals.

Jessica chose *Article1st* to search for articles.

TOPIC AREA: All Databases
__NO.__DATABASE_____DESCRIPTION_____
|
| 1 WorldCat   Books and other materials in libraries worldwide.
| 2 Article1st Index of articles from nearly 12,500 journals.
| 3 Contents1st Table of contents of nearly 12,500 journals.
|_____

HINTS: Select a database . . . . type database number or name. Help on a database . . . . type H and database name.   Return to Topic Area screen . . . . just press Enter.

ACTIONS: Help BYE Reset

DATABASE NUMBER (or Action):Trying 128.175.83.3 . . .
Connected to poole.lib. uXyz.edu.
Escape character is ' ^]'.

Using Article1st, Jessica located several articles in journals that her library did not own. She arranged to borrow them through an interlibrary loan.

In addition to Article1st, there are also commercial services that will download articles directly to your terminal for a fee. One of those is CARL UnCover. Jessica decided to look for articles in that database. (If you choose a commercial service, be careful, because fees can mount quickly.)

University of XYZ Library (poole.lib.uXyz.edu)

Trying 192.54.81.120 . . .
Connected to 192.54.81.120.
Escape character is ' ^]'.
Trying 8021000003 . . . Open
Welcome to the CARL system
Please identify your terminal. Choices are:
1.ADM (all)
2.APPLE,IBM
3.TANDEM
4.TELE-914
5.VT100 (terminal type is often VT100)

(Check with your computing center to discover your terminal type.)

6.WYSE 50
7.ZENTEC
8.HARDCOPY
9.IBM 316x
Use HARDCOPY if your terminal type isn't listed...
SELECT LINE #:
> > Welcome to the UnCover Standard Internet Gateway < < <

1. UnCover—Article Access and Delivery
2. CARL Corporation Database Services
58. British Library Document Supply Centre

*******NEW DATABASE******* ?U for more information

99. UnCover EXPRESS (Articles Delivered within 1 hour)

* UnCover is a database of current article information taken
from more than 17,000 multidisciplinary journals. UnCover
contains brief descriptive information about over
7,000,000 articles which have appeared since Fall 1988.

* UnCover is easy to use, with keyword access to article titles
and summaries. You can also "recreate" the tables of contents
pages from journals of particular interest to you.

You may enter //EXIT at any time to leave this system.
Enter the NUMBER of your choice, and press the <RETURN> key >

UnCover is a periodical index and document delivery service. In order
to make it easier for you to select and order articles of interest, you
may want to create an UnCover PROFILE. If you want to use the UnCover
Reveal service, you must set up an UnCover PROFILE which includes your
e-mail address and payment information.

This PROFILE information (name, e-mail address, fax number, etc.) will be
saved and may be used each time you use UnCover. Your PROFILE can be
edited whenever you choose to do so.

If you do not wish to set up a PROFILE at this time, you may still search
the UnCover database and order articles. It will be necessary for you to
enter payment and delivery information with each order you place.

Type NEW to CREATE a new profile
Type EDIT to MODIFY current profile
Type ?R for a description of the UnCover REVEAL service
Type ORDERINFO for ORDER STATUS and FUND balances
Press

Keywords   Generating effective keywords takes practice. Usually, students
begin the quest with very broad and general terms. For example, if they are
searching for information on *drug abuse,* they might search under that term.
Sometimes they find hundreds of articles and are overwhelmed with the
sheer mass of information. Other times, they get frustrated because they
can't find anything.

*The trick is to make a list of synonyms for your topic, making the list
more and more specific as you go.* For example, articles about *drug abuse*
may be found by searching for the name of a particular drug such as *heroin*
or *cocaine* or *marijuana* or *alcohol.* Also, be sure to make a list of variant

forms of your search term. If you are looking for information about children's rights, you might need to search under *child and rights* rather than *children.* Remember: Computers can't think. All they can do is match patterns. They are not clever at all, but you are!

:-> :-) **Try This** :-O ;-)

Generate a List of Keywords   Start with the general term for a topic of interest to you and practice listing possible search terms. For example, if you are interested in the preservation of national parks, you might start with *national parks,* then go to a specific park such as *Yellowstone,* or even a specific attraction within the park such as *Old Faithful,* or a specific animal within the park such as *elk.* Then you could combine the terms using Boolean operators.

If you are not sure of the form of the word you want to search, for example drug or drug(s), try truncating or shortening your terms by using an asterisk, *, after the root of the word. Example: vegeta* retrieves references to "vegetable," "vegetables," "vegetation,"and so forth.

KEEPING RECORDS: KEYWORDS

The secret to doing an efficient, effective research project is record-keeping. For example, as you search, *keep a careful list of the keywords you use.* If you don't, you are likely to forget which ones you searched and repeat them again and again.

Keeping a record of keywords will also show you which words were effective and which were not. Note the number of hits you received on a particular keyword. If you are searching an online card catalog (OPAC), notice the suggested subject headings listed on the screen when you find a source. For example, if you search under child abuse, you will probably find "see also" terms such as *adolescents, parents and abuse, rehabilitation,* and *recovery* at the bottom of the page on which you find a book or journal.

Make a note of these suggested search terms in your notebook or in an online file.

You can use your record to help you focus and narrow your topic. If, for example, you search under *violence and sports* and find hundreds of articles, you know your search must be narrowed. In general, if you find more than forty hits for a particular term, try narrowing and focusing. For example, instead of using *sports and violence,* you might try a particular sport or a particular kind of injury.

Boolean Operators   If you search the Internet (or even the OPAC for your library) using broad terms such as *campus crime,* you will probably get hundreds of "hits," but most of them will not be useful.

To develop useful keyword search strategies on computers, you should learn to use Boolean operators such as *and, or,* and *not* to combine terms.

For example, if you search for *campus crime and sexual assault,* you will get just a few references, but many of them are likely to be useful if you are focusing your paper specifically on the issue of sexual assaults.

On the other hand, if you get too few hits on a topic, you can broaden your search by using *or* to combine terms. For example, if you are searching for information under the terms *college crime and rape* and get too few responses, you can use *college crime and (rape or sexual assault).* That way, you will pick up references under either term.

If you are getting too much information, you can also narrow the search term by using the Boolean operator *not.* For example, if you want to look at types of assaults on college campuses that are *not* sexual, then you might search under *college crime and assault not sexual.*

:-> :-) **Try This** :-O ;-)

Choose a Topic You Are Interested in and Develop a Keyword Search Strategy Using Boolean Operators   First, try using a broad search strategy by looking under the general topic, for example, *recycling,* and recording the number of hits. Then narrow your terms by combining your subject with another related term. For example, *recycling and cost* or *recycling and benefits.* Record the number of hits and examine the types of sources. Are you finding some scholarly works? If you are not getting a sufficient number of hits, broaden your search by combining terms with *or.* For example, *recycling or landfills.* Finally, narrow the search even further by using *not:* for example, you might search under *recycling not newspapers.* Report the results of your experience with Boolean operators on the class listserv. Compare your results with the results of others. What kinds of strategies seem to work best?

OPACS: ONLINE PUBLIC ACCESS CATALOGS

Probably your school has put its card catalog online. If so, you will find several advantages, as well as some disadvantages, compared to the old paper-based system of 3 × 5 cards.

Advantages: Keyword searches allow you to combine terms, saving a great deal of time over the old subject-based or author/title searches. Because you can combine terms, you can make your search much more specific than in the past (see information about Boolean searches on p. 106). If you have modem access or if your computer is hardwired to the mainframe, you can search the library's holdings without leaving the comfort of your home or residence hall. Often you can even print out a search and carry the print-out to the stacks of the library. Read the information carefully. Many systems tell you, for example, if a book is checked out or on reserve; some also tell you if a collection of journals is at the bindery.

Disadvantages: Because OPACs are human creations, sometimes there are errors or omissions. If your library has both a traditional card catalog and an OPAC, try to check both systems—especially if your topic requires searching for older sources. Sometimes OPACS do not list sources before a particular date. Check with your local librarian to be sure.

:-> :-) **Try This** :-O ;-)

Search Your Library's OPAC for Five Sources for Your Research Paper   Use keywords to make your search as specific as possible. Focus your search by using terms suggested at the bottom of the screen. If your OPAC lists both books and journals, try finding two or three books by creditable authors; then look for journal titles for articles you have found by searching the Internet or looking in CD-ROM databases (see p. 107). For example, if your topic is *computers in the classroom,* and you found an article called "Computers Meet Classroom: Classroom Wins," in a journal called the *Teachers' College Record,* search your OPAC under the journal title to see if there is a copy in the stacks. Keep a record of your search, including authors, titles, and call numbers, and post the results to your class listserv. Compare your results with the results of others—especially those doing a similar topic. If several students list the same sources, make a plan to share the sources, rather than compete for them.

After searching the card catalog, use some online indexes to periodicals such as CD-ROM databases.

COMPILE AN ANNOTATED CLASS RESEARCH DATABASE

If all members of the class share the results of their online searches, you can create a rich, searchable resource. First record the bibliographic information about each item. (See Appendix A for information on citing online sources.) Then write a sentence or two describing the strengths and weaknesses of the source. Finally, post your bibliography on e-mail, or to a class folder on the local area network (LAN).

CD-ROM Databases   Many periodicals such as magazines, journals, and newspapers, are indexed on CD-ROM databases. At some schools, you must be at the library to use these CDS; at others, you can access a package of

CD-ROMs networked on a Gopher or a home page on the WWW. Check your campus experts to see how to access databases that index periodicals.

:-> :-) **Try This** :-O ;-)

When You Have Discovered How to Access Electronic Indexes to Periodicals, Find Three Articles for Your Research Paper   Here are some hints to help you find the best articles.

1. *Choose a database that is appropriate to your topic.* Some are very general; others cover one subject in detail. Indexes useful for composition students include *Searchbank,* which lists articles in the *Expanded Academic Index* from 1980 to the present; the *Business Index,* which has references, abstracts, or full text of articles from more than nine hundred business, management, economics, industry, and trade publications from 1982 to the present; and the *National Newspaper Index,* which includes references to articles published in the *New York Times, Christian Science Monitor, Wall Street Journal, Los Angeles Times,* and *Washington Post* for the past three years. You may also find *PsycInfo* useful if you are doing a paper that is related to human relationships or growth and development.

2. *Identify search terms and concepts.* For example, if you were doing a paper on bilingual education for Native Americans, your list of search terms might include *Native Americans, bilingual education,* and *language policy.* You might also include a list of particular tribes such as *Navajo* or *Apache.* Brainstorm possible search terms for your topic.

3. *Use Boolean operators to combine terms.* For example, you might search for *Navajo and bilingual education.*

4. *Download your results to disk or print them out.* To learn how to download or print from your system, ask your reference librarian. Increasingly databases include abstracts or the full text of articles. If this is the case, you will have your material in a handy format.

5. *If the text of articles themselves is not included in the database, consult your OPAC under the name of the journal to see if your library has it.* If not, consult Interlibrary Loan to see if you can obtain a copy of the article from another library.

CREATE A DATABANK OF ONLINE SURVEYS AND INTERVIEWS

Share data from surveys and interviews conducted in the class listserv or other listservs or Usenet groups in a central file where all members of the class can use it for research papers.

Gophers: OCLC and CARL UnCover   When you have finished searching your local library, try launching out on your journey for the gold. In addition to the OPAC catalog and local databases, venture into cyberspace and use Gopher to "go to" other libraries and online indexes of periodicals on the Internet.

:-> :-) **T r y   T h i s** :-O ;-)

Use Gopher to Locate Some Sources for Your Research Paper   Ask your local computing experts or your librarian how to access your school's Gopher, a menu-driven system that links information and resources usable by those who don't have access to the WWW.

Using Gopher, visit three sources of information for your paper and record the results of your search. For example, you might go to a library at another location, such as The Online Card Catalog of the Library of Congress (OCLC), is a valuable resource because it lists nearly everything published in the United States. It's definitely worth a try. It also lists where you can obtain a copy of a particular book from Interlibrary Loan. When you have found three sources on the Gopher, post your results to your class listserv and compare your results to those of your classmates.

RECORD KEEPING: WORKING BIBLIOGRAPHY

As you find sources in the online card catalog or on the Internet or the WWW, make a note of the information you will need for your Works Cited page or to find the source again.

For *books,* records the author, title, place of publishing, name of publisher, and date of publication. It's also a good idea to record the call number.

For *articles,* record the title of the article, the name of the journal, the volume and issue, the date of publication, and the page numbers.

For *online information,* note if you are using e-mail or a listserv or the WWW. Also note authors, titles, dates, and most especially—e-mail addresses or URLs. Since information on the Internet changes frequently, it is especially important to record dates.

For more detailed information about documenting online sources see page 167.

Telnet and FTP   Before the World Wide Web was created, researchers used Telnet to log on to computer systems in remote locations. Then they used FTP (file transfer protocol) to transfer documents found on the remote system. If your school has access to the WWW, you probably don't need to use

Telnet and FTP. If not, ask your local experts or librarian how to use Telnet and FTP on your school's mainframe computer system.

:-> :-) **Try This** :-O ;-)

Use Telnet to "Travel"   Using the instructions supplied by your local experts, log on to your school's mainframe system and use Telnet to "travel" to another institution. When you reach the other site, log on to the host computer. If you are asked for a password, try using "guest" or "anonymous."

While you are visiting the remote computer, browse through the resources. Try to find at least two resources for your paper. When you find your resource, download it from your mainframe account to your personal computer by using instructions from your local experts. If the file is "compressed," decompress it using the instructions provided on your campus. When you have finished using Telnet and FTP, report the results of your experience to your classmates on the listserv.

Surfing the Web—Don't Get Drowned!   By far the most powerful way to find information on the Internet is by using the resources of the Web. Using a "browser" such as Netscape or Internet Explorer, or a search engine such as Webcrawler, AltaVista, or Yahoo! you can find tons of information quickly.

If you are working at a remote location using a modem, find out what software you need to connect to the Web. Since the Web is highly graphical, you will need software that can support graphics. Once you have installed the connection software, try jumping into the surf. First do some exploring. Then use a browser to locate information on your research topic. To open a browser, double-click your mouse on the icon for a search engine and follow the instructions on the screen.

For most browsers, you should click on the box where you fill in a search term and use Boolean operators to combine terms.

< @ HOME PAGE OF THE LIBRARY OF CONGRESS :-<

If you have WWW access, browse the home page for the national library at http://lcweb.loc.gov/homepage/lchp.html. This resource is full of excellent, up-to-date information. If you are interested in legislation pending in Congress, you can find the text of bills by choosing THOMAS: Legislative Information at the Library of Congress home page. You can also get access under Research Tools to the card catalogs of many libraries.

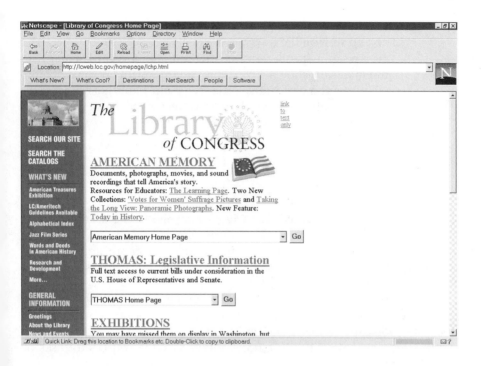

FINDING SOURCES ONLINE

In the following e-mail exchange, two students talk about finding sources on the Net for their papers. Ashley gives Sarah good advice.

From: Ashley Marie Booth <ashleyb@xyzu.edu>

To: Sarah Margar Wilson <sarahw@xyzu.edu>

Subject: Re: foreign language requirement

On Thu, 14 Nov 1996, Sarah Margar Wilson wrote:

> Hi!- I'm doing my paper on making foreign language a require-
> ment in high school. I was having trouble finding sources about
> my topic. The books that I found were all on bilingual educa-
> tion, not on foreign language requirement. Could someone
> please write back and tell me their opinion on this topic? I'm
> not sure just yet who my audience is, so if I get some feedback
> from someone it will probably make my decision a little easier.
> Also, could you please tell me a good place to look for my
> sources because books just aren't working for me. Thanks a lot.
> -Sarah

Hi, Sarah

Look up stuff on the Internet, it's really helpful. Go to Webcrawler and type in a search word, something like foreign language requirements in schools. I tried this yesterday with my topic of bilingual education and Native Americans and found lots of journals that were online. The whole articles were there, so all you have to do is print them out. Good Luck!

-Ashley

:-> :-) Try This :-O ;-)

Do a Search for Three Online Sources   Open one of the search engines such as Yahoo! or AltaVista and click on the box where you fill in a search term. Use Boolean operators to combine terms. If you are not successful with one set of keywords, try using another. Successful searches generate a *manageable* number of results.

Make a record of the URLs (universal resource locators, or Internet addresses) of the resources you have found. If you are working on your own computer, you can save these sites as bookmarks (see p. 114). If you are at a public site, record the URLs in a notebook or save the sources to disks by downloading.

While you are browsing, *critically evaluate the sites.* Which look like advertisements? Which seem like one-sided propaganda? Which have information only? Which have explanation or analysis? Record each site with comments. Share your results with the class.

URLs   URLs, or universal resource locators, are addresses for sites on the World Wide Web. All URLs begin with *http://;* this is the *hypertext transfer protocol.* The protocol is followed by the *domain name,* usually *www. nameofcollege.edu* (or *businessname.com* or *organizationname.org).* After the domain name, you may find a forward slash (/) followed by the directory path. For example, if you wished to visit the English department site at the University of XYZ, the address might be http://www.xyzu.edu/english.

:-> :-) Try This :-O ;-)

Visit Ten Web Sites and List Their URLs, Which Appear at the Top of the Home Page   Analyze your list. What kinds of domain names did you find? Do you see any pattern to the domain names and the directory paths? Record sites you found useful in your notebook or online. Share your results with your classmates.

RECORD THIS INFORMATION ABOUT INTERNET SOURCES

Author

Title

Electronic address

Date of publication

Date of access

Part or section heading or number

Other important info—e-mail, Usenet, home page, and so forth

Browsers: Navigator, Internet Explorer   Software programs called "browsers," which display video and graphics and play sound, allow you to explore the Web. If you have access to a browser from a lab, ask your computer site coordinator how to use it. Generally, these browsers are point-and-click style. You simply use the mouse to choose the browser you want to use; then type in a keyword and begin a search. To learn how to use them, jump in and see what you find. After a few tries, you will discover if your terms are too broad or too narrow. All of the browsers have Help buttons. Use the Help function if you are feeling lost.

If you are using a computer at home with a modem, you will need a PPP (point-to-point protocol) or SLIP (serial line Internet protocol) connection. Check with your school to see how to set up a connection to the Web from your home computer.

If your school does not offer SLIP or PPP connections, you can still get access to the Web from your home computer by subscribing to a commercial service such as America Online, Compuserve, Prodigy, or the Microsoft Network. You can also check your phone book for local Internet service providers. For one fee, they offer access to e-mail and the Web as well as other Internet services.

:-> :-) Try This :-O ;-)

Compare Browsers   If you have access to two or more browsers, search all of them for your topic and compare the results. Which browser did you find easiest to use? Which provided the most useful results? Share your results with your classmates.

Subject Trees: Yahoo!, Einet Galaxy, Clearinghouse   Some search engines are especially well suited to academic research—particularly those with subject-tree directories. In these directories, subjects have been grouped into categories such as the arts, business and economics, computers and the Internet, education, science, and so forth. If you need help focusing and narrowing your topic, try a subject-tree search engine such as Yahoo! (Yahoo.com), Clearinghouse (www/clearinghouse.net), Infomine (lib-www.ucr.edu), or Internet Public Library (www.ipl.org), Einet Galaxy (www.einet.net), or Excite (www.excite.com).

:-> :-) **Try This** :-O ;-)

Compare Subject-Tree Engines   Take a general subject such as the *environment* and use two of the search engines to narrow and focus your topic. Keep a record of your search. Compare the two search engines. What similarities and differences do you find? Which did the better job for you? Share your results with your classmates on the class listserv.

Bookmarks   So that you can find a site easily and quickly the next time you want to visit it, get into the habit of making bookmarks. Look at the menus on your browser and find the Bookmark menu. *If you are working at a public site, you may have to save the bookmarks to a disk or they will be erased the next time you visit.* Consult the site assistant to see how to save bookmarks.

:-> :-) **Try This** :-O ;-)

Working with Bookmarks   Visit three sites for your research paper and save the URL for each one in a bookmark. Copy the bookmarks onto a floppy disk or copy and paste them into your word processor document. If several students are working on the same topic, share your bookmarks with others.

Evaluating Sources   Researchers have always found difficulty evaluating source material. Whom do you trust on your journey for the gold? Who are the reliable, accurate, up-to-date guides to signposts along the way? Who are the scabs and scallywags who tell you about false lodes and deliberately lead you away from the gold they may wish to keep for themselves?

In the past, researchers have relied on verifiable data such as biographical information about the author of a source (who is this person, what has she done with her life), information about the publisher (a university press), or a well-known journal or newspaper, or a solid list of works cited. Researchers have asked themselves if the information presented in the source seems to be *vague and ambiguous* or *factual and verifiable.* Does the source seem fair and unbiased? Does it present both sides of an issue? Does the author or creator of the sources make his or her *assumptions* clear? Is the author aware of a *bias?* Is the source *logical and coherent?* Are the conclusions drawn from the evidence *reasonable?* Is the material *clear?* Is the source *consistent?* Does the author acknowledge what is hard data and what is *theory* or *inference?* Does the author accept the factual claims of others without fully investigating them? Does the author's treatment of the subject *reflect the subject matter?* For example, anecdotal evidence may work in the humanities, but is it suitable for the sciences? Even in the humanities, it is important to ask yourself the *size of the sample* that the author studied.

In the case of Internet sources, all of the above questions are important, but sometimes it is difficult to tell, because of the fluid and somewhat democratic nature of the medium, which sources are reliable, accurate, and complete. Since nearly anyone can put up a Web page or join a Usenet talk group, many more people can "publish" than in the past. In the past, if an author wished to publish a scholarly article, he or she had to submit it to a journal. Then the article was read by "referees" who judged its scholarliness. If the journal accepted it for publication, it was generally trustworthy. Now, articles are often published on the Internet without anyone verifying reliability or accuracy. Therefore, as an online researcher, it is important that you scrutinize source material closely.

In the case of a Web page, look for a *sponsoring organization* or an *author.* If you discover the author or sponsor, look for *credentials* that establish the authority of the individual or organization. Who are these people? Are they *biased* in any way? Is there a *goal* or *mission statement* on the source material? Is there a *FAQ file* that gives background information about the author or organization? What is the *purpose* for the site? Is it a commercial site that is attempting to *sell a product or promote a cause?* Do the texts at the site *present a balanced point of view?* Are there many sides to the discussion? Do the *multimedia effects such as sound or graphics confuse the message?*

:-> :-) **Try This** :-O ;-)

Evaluate Sources on the WWW   Using the criteria given above (reliability, accuracy, bias, purpose, commercialization, distractions, etc.), visit two or three Web pages on a topic of your choice. Evaluate each page according to its usefulness as a potential source for a research paper. For example, if your topic is *pornography and its effects on children,* use a search engine such as AltaVista or Yahoo! to visit several Web sites on this issue. Make some notes about each page. Record the URL, the date visited, the name of the author of the site or the sponsoring organization, and generally describe the material found there. Does the site seem to present all points of view on the issue, or is it merely propaganda for one side or another? Are opinions backed up by verifiable statistics or evidence? Or is the material biased and anecdotal? Is there a religious or political bias? When you have finished examining some sites, compile your observations and post a message to the class listserv reviewing the sites as possible sources for research papers.

Plagiarism   When writing a research paper, using traditional sources or the Internet, you should always avoid *plagiarism*—using the words or ideas of others without citing the source. Because of the nature of the Internet—whether on e-mail, on a listserv, or browsing through pages on the WWW—writers often feel involved in a group discussion. It's easy to lose track of who said what, and ideas often seem like the product of a shared effort. But if you keep careful records of e-mail correspondence or listserv threads of discussion, Usenet groups, or home pages visited, you will have no trouble giving proper credit to the author.

Above all, avoid the temptation to copy and paste source material into your paper and treat it as though it was your own work. This is a serious violation of academic ethics and could result in severe penalties from your college or university. Acquaint yourself with your student handbook and with the section on plagiarism and documentation in your English handbook. If you respect ideas and words as the personal property of the owner-author, you will have no trouble with plagiarism. If you have any doubts about whether material found online should be cited, and how, check the section in this chapter on documentation or ask your instructor.

:-> :-) Try This :-O ;-)

Summarize and Paraphrase   Open one of your directories of stored e-mail and *practice summarizing and paraphrasing* the material so that you can use it (with proper citation) in an essay of your own. For example, if you have a directory called Austen (you have been participating in online discussions of the films based on the novels of Jane Austen, *Sense and Sensibility* and *Emma*), you might have several messages debating which of the films comes closer to conveying the sense of the novel or the sense of country life in eighteenth-century England.

Choose four or five of the most interesting messages (the ones with the best illustrations, examples, and supports), and paste them into a file you have created with a word processor. Save this file. Next, *highlight* the most interesting words, phrases or sentences with bold or underlining. (These you may want to quote directly in your own essay.) *Make a copy of the file* and experiment with summarizing and paraphrasing messages. Look back at the rest of the material. Which words can simply be cut? Which passages repeat the ideas of others? Which passages can be summarized in a sentence or two or paraphrased (put into your own words)?

Experiment with several ways of treating the material. Save each version in a separate file for later comparison. Cut unnecessary words and redundancies. After you have practice summarizing and paraphrasing, try blending this source material into an essay of your own. Use the material to support your opinions or to provide substance for debate. Do you, for example, agree or disagree with Writer X that *Emma* is a much more engaging film than *Sense and Sensibility* and that it brings eighteenth-century England to life in a convincing manner? Or do you disagree?

Copyright Issues Students have always been concerned with plagiarism issues when writing research papers, but now you must also be concerned with violating *copyright*.

With plagiarism, you should avoid using the words or ideas of another person without proper attribution—without citing the source in your text and listing it on a Works Cited page.

Using print sources, you might analyze a song lyric, citing the source with the author, title, and page number, and that would be fine. But if you put that song lyric in your paper and then post your paper on the Web (see Chapter 5 for information on creating Web pages of your own), you would be publishing to the world. That is a violation of the copyright laws. Why is this illegal? Because by putting the song on the Net (perhaps even inserting the sound of the song itself by digitizing the sound), you may be depriving the composer of money. Instead of buying a recording of the song, someone who reads your essay online could download the song for free.

< @ >   COPYRIGHT: WORDS VS. IDEAS :-> :-<

You need permission to quote only copyrighted words. Ideas cannot be copyrighted. If you *summarize or paraphrase* any online material, you do not need permission to use it (you should, however, acknowledge the source), but words—even e-mail—are copy-protected.

To stay on the safe side of copyright, follow the *Fair Use Guidelines* on page 118.

:-> :-) Try This :-O ;-)

Investigate Your School's Policy On Plagiarism Find out what constitutes plagiarism at your school. What is the penalty for plagiarism? Then investigate the policy for copyright violation. Does your school have a clear statement on

> ## ‹ @ › FAIR USE OF COPYRIGHTED MATERIAL › ‹
>
> 1. You can quote excerpts of *300 words* from a book or *150 words* from a magazine or newspaper article if:
>   *The excerpt is not a complete unit in the larger work*—for example, a poem in a magazine, a chapter in a book, an article in a newspaper, or a list of rules in a manual.
>   *The excerpt makes up less than 20 percent* of the total words in the source.
>   *The excerpted words are integrated into your own work* and do not stand alone.
>   You give *full credit* to the author, source, and publisher.
> 2. *If you quote several short passages from a source and they total more than the allowable amount (300 words for a book or 150 words from a magazine or newspaper), you must get permission from the author or the publisher.*
>   Often you can get permission for materials found on the Internet by writing e-mail to the author.
>
> **Note:** This is *not* a legal definition of fair use. Interpretations of fair use change frequently. If you intend to publish your essay on the Web, consult the Fair Use Web site for the latest interpretation of policy (*http://www.libraries.psu.edu/avs/fairuse*).

use of materials from the Internet in your research papers? When you have a clear understanding of your school's policy on these issues, post a note to the class list. Compare your understanding to the understanding of others in the class. Is there a difference of opinion among your classmates regarding the interpretation of your school's policy, or is there agreement?

When you have finished investigating your school's policy on plagiarism and copyright violations, visit some Web sites on the issue. One interesting site is The Copyright Website (*http://www.benedict.com/*). At this site you can learn about copyright fundamentals, famous copyright infringements, Internet issues, the fair use law and public domain. After you have visited this site, write an argument for or against clearer laws for copyright issues on the Web.

Developing a Thesis   After you have narrowed and focused your topic and found some source material that examines both sides of the issue, it's time to develop a thesis. A thesis is a specific, arguable statement about your topic—a statement that somebody could disagree with. A thesis takes a stand. For example, in the following e-mail messages, Kristy helps Heather finds a thesis on the topic of child abuse:

On Thu, 14 Nov 1996, Heather D'Agostino wrote:

I'm doing my research paper on child abuse. I haven't been exactly sure about what I want my thesis to say. Maybe you can help. I want to see which has a worse effect on people in the long run, mental or physical abuse. I'm going to start my paper with an anecdote. It will hopefully interest the reader and encourage them to read on. Then I will state some facts and statistics about child abuse. Then I will compare and contrast the effects of child abuse once the victims are grown. What do you think?

From: Kristy Lynn Redford <klr@xyzu.edu>

To: Heather D'Agostino <hdag@xyzu.edu>

Subject: Re: Child Abuse

For your thesis, you could take the angle that physical scars only last a week or two, but emotional scars last a lifetime. It leaves the child growing up with almost no self-esteem, but a lot of aggression. You could also talk about whether or not victims of child abuse grow up to be abusers themselves because all of this aggression has built-up through the years.

Or you could talk about why most children do not tell anyone of their abuse.

Kristy's suggestions were helpful. Heather did decide to argue that the emotional scars of child abuse are worse than the physical scars. She cited evidence pro and con, interviewed some victims of child abuse, and joined a Usenet group on the topic.

:-> :-) **Try This** :-O ;-)

Find a Thesis   Examine your source material on a topic of choice and list some debatable statements. Choose the statement that interests you most and create a thesis for your paper. Share your process in the class listserv, then play devil's advocate online to sharpen your argument. Ask your classmates to role-play a particular audience. Then try to convince that audience that your view is right. They should try to find holes in your argument and challenge you to defend your position.

Using Sources to Support an Argument   When writing a research paper, use sources to support your own ideas. Do not just paste material together in a sort of collage and call it a research paper.

Whether you are writing a traditional, linear paper or a hypertext (see Chapter 5, page 131), you need to have a thesis—a controlling idea. And you need to think through the logic of that thesis and look at the topic from all sides. You also need to be prepared to examine the opposing side of the issue. In fact, the strongest arguments acknowledge that the other side has some good points and that some compromise might be possible in some areas.

Use your sources to support your points, not as a substitute for original thinking. For example, you might use some statistics or data or an expert opinion or a highly original and interesting quote to back up your opinions.

:-> :-) Try This :-O ;-)

Using Source Materials   After you have done some prewriting and developed keywords on your topic, search online for articles in scholarly publications, books, periodicals, or Web pages. You might also participate in a listserv or a Usenet group and save interesting posts. Then, based on the evidence that you have found and tested, *develop a thesis*—an arguable stand on your topic—and *develop a plan* or *outline,* paying attention to both sides of the issue. After you have developed your plan, look again at your source material and evaluate each item. *Which of the sources will you quote?* In general, a research paper should have no more than 10 percent quoted material, no more than two or three block quotes. Which sources will you *summarize* in a sentence or two? Which ones will you *paraphrase* into your own words? Present your plan for using your source materials to your instructor or your classmates. Which points need stronger support?

Documenting Online Sources   Keep good records of all of your sources for your papers, but especially the sources you find on the Internet. Because millions of people can post information online, be sure to note authors, publishing organizations, and so forth. And because information changes daily, it is important to note URLs and dates when you visit a site. For complete information on forms of documentation, see Appendix A.

:-> :-) Try This :-O ;-)

Prepare a List of Works Cited   for your research paper, listing the materials found on the Internet (listservs, Usenet groups, Gopher, WWW, and so forth). To find the correct form for citations, see Appendix A.

Details! Details!   Sometimes students have concerns about the format of a paper or ways to integrate sources.

Read the following e-mail messages from Ashley, one of the students in my composition course, and think about your paper. Do you have similar questions for your instructor?

From: Ashley Marie Booth <ashleyb@xyzu.edu>

To: EDickinson@amherst.edu

Subject: Number of Sources

Hi Ms. Dickinson:
How many sources do we need to have for our research paper, or isn't there a requirement? I just found three helpful articles from journals on the Internet. Thanks for telling me about that! Also, do we have to have the whole draft ready for tomorrow?
Thank You,

To: Ashley

From: EDickinson

Re: sources

I suggest five sources for a 6-8 page paper. With that many, you usually have enough information to present both sides of an issue.

From: Ashley Marie Booth <ashleyb@xyzu.edu>

To: Emily Dickinson <EDickinson@amherst.edu>

Subject: quotes

Hi Ms. Dickinson:
I have a list of things that I want to put in my paper, Should I block them and paraphrase them, or list them 1-6?
thanks-
Ashley

From: Emily Dickinson <EDickinson@amherst.edu>

To: Ashley Marie Booth <ashleyb@xyzu.edu>

Subject: Re: quotes

Hi Ashley,
Well . . . it depends. Are the individual items in the list long or short? If they are short, just quote them, treating them like any block quote.
If they are long, paraphrase them and cite the source.
Hope this helps. If you want to stop by, I'll be in my office today from 9-12 and 1:30-3.

From: Ashley Marie Booth <ashleyb@xyzu.edu>

To: Emily Dickinson <EDickinson@amherst.edu>

Subject: block quotes

Hi again!
Should these quotes be single or double spaced?
Thank you,
Ashley

From: Emily Dickinson<EDickinson@amherst.edu>

To: Ashley Marie Booth <ashleyb@xyzu.edu>

Subject: Re: Spacing

Hi Ashley,
The WHOLE paper should be double-spaced. That's new since the
advent of word processors. Just turn on double spacing and leave
it on.
Cheers,

From: Ashley Marie Booth <ashleyb@xyzu.edu>

To: Emily Dickinson <EDickinson@amherst.edu>

Subject: sources

Hi Ms. Dickinson:
Do we have to quote from all of our sources?
Thanks,
Ashley

From: Emily Dickinson <EDickinson@amherst.edu>

To: Ashley Marie Booth <ashleyb@xyzu.edu>

Subject: Re: sources and other issues

Hi Ashley,
You ask GREAT questions!!!
No, you do not have to quote from all your sources, but if you don't
quote, you should paraphrase or summarize from them. The list is
called Works Cited; that means you actually used them in your text.
If you have some sources that you think are excellent on the subject, but you did not use them in your paper itself, you can add a
list of Works Consulted. That means you looked at them, and they
were good—perhaps for background info—but you did not actually cite them in your paper.
PS I bet you're doing a great job!

From: Ashley Marie Booth <ashleyb@xyzu.edu>

To: Emily Dickinson <EDickinson@amherst.edu>

Subject: citing

Yet another question from Ashley!
I want to take a quote from a book, but the chapter that it is in is written by another author. How do I cite this? Thank you!
Ashley

From: Emily Dickinson <EDickinson@amherst.edu>

To: Ashley Marie Booth <ashleyb@xyzu.edu>

Subject: Re: citing

Hi Ashley,
Is this a collection of essays with an editor (sounds like it)? If so, in the list of Works Cited, list the whole book under the name of the *editor* (see the handbook for form of citation). Then, also list the name of the essay under the author who wrote it: for example, if the editor of the collection was named Brown and the author of the essay was named Smith, list the book under Brown, ed. and the essay under Smith, "Title of Essay." Then put the name of the editor, Brown, and list the page numbers of the essay by Smith.
The form is in the handbook, but if you're still stuck, please see me before or after class, and I'll try to explain it more clearly.

SAMPLE STUDENT ESSAY

When Nancy Matthews became intrigued by the amount of publicity about the use of computers in education, she was not sure where she stood on the issue, but she knew she wanted to think it through. Therefore, this was an ideal topic for her to explore for a research paper.

Online, she found President Bill Clinton's executive order titled "Ensuring Technology: Ensuring Opportunity For All Children in the Next Century." This was her starting point. As she investigated more sources, both on- and offline—scholarly works as well as popular materials—Nancy found that although little has been published reporting solid success teaching with technology, schools, encouraged by the top leadership in business and government, seem to feel hard-pressed to implement technology in the classroom as soon as possible. *Nancy began to feel that she had a real audience and real purpose, and her voice became strong. She felt challenged to answer those who would use her hard-earned tax dollars and the children of this country as guinea pigs in an experiment.*

Read Nancy's paper and look for ways she has used her voice to speak directly to those in power to make decisions. Do you think her voice is effective in this paper? Why or why not? Does she force you to listen to her side, even if you disagree with her? To back up your opinion of Nancy's voice, point to particular words, phrases, or sentences in her essay. What is her tone? Describe her voice. Is it confident and assertive or strident and aggressive? How do you know? How has she used her sources to back up her argument? Are her sources well chosen for her paper? Why, or why not?

< @ > :-) :-"COMPUTER FRENZY" :O :-> :-<

By Nancy E. Matthews

It is becoming a popular belief that in this century, it will be critical to be digital. But is this necessarily true? As a result of this belief, many efforts are being made to integrate the use of computers in schools. President Bill Clinton has said that in the year 2,000 every classroom will have Internet-linked computers so that "... American children [will have] the skills they need to succeed in the information-intensive 21st century ..." (677). It's time to ask some important questions. For example: on what basis do authorities feel that the use of computers will be beneficial to students? There has been no definite proof that there is educational merit for these new technologies (Dvorak 85). It seems that many citizens have major impulses to change schools through technology. It is evident that administrators and other technology craving citizens have not thought through the negative aspects of computers in education. The fact is that extensive and primary use of computers in education can be detrimental to the social environment of a classroom the teacher-student relationship, and the importance of collaborative learning.

Larry Cuban, author of "Computers Meet Classroom: Classroom Wins," believes that there are three significant reasons why administrators are in so much of a hurry to metamorphosize schools through technology. The first reason is the drive to bring schools in step with the workplace (189). "Employees who are adept at technology earn 10 to 15 percent higher pay," according to Alan Krueger, chief economist for the U.S. Labor Department" (qtd in Hancock 50). It is true that, in the future, wages for computer literate workers will rise and wages for unskilled workers will fall. But the solution to this phenomenon is not to introduce computers in elementary schools. Computers are not like musical instruments which take many years of practice to master. As technology improves, so does the friendlier use of computers. It is becoming easier and easier to operate computers successfully without prior access. Consequently, many experts dealing with computers in their professions were not exposed to the advanced equipment at young ages. According to Cuffaro, "It is when children move more firmly into functioning at the concrete operational level, at about age eight, that they are better able to take true advantages of the challenges that computers and programming may offer" (27).

This brings to mind Cuban's second point: loss of self-directed learning (189). If children's capacity to imagine is corrupted by video games, television, and interactive computer software, their creative nature will eventually deteriorate (Cuffaro 37). They may also filter out essential mechanics in cognitive skills such as basic mathematics and grammar. Most word processing programs include features such as spell checkers and grammar checkers; if young people use them to write, they will eventually realize that learning basic grammar and spelling is irrelevant if the computer will do the work for them. And what about the use of calculators or math-based computer programs? The simplicity of punching in numbers on a machine to receive the correct answer is faster and easier than figuring work out by hand. Children will, therefore, never learn the basic steps needed for accomplishing higher mathematics successfully if they rely on calculators. They may not master important skills used in further cognitive learning, stunting their educational growth.

Cuban's third point touches on the impulse for productivity of "teaching more in less time" (189). Computers do not get exhausted and they do not request a raise in pay or benefits; therefore, to an administrator they seem to be the ideal tool. But what happens when benefactors pay enormous sums of money to fund computers in schools and something new comes out which performs faster, better, and cheaper? Computers are expensive and require constant upgrading and maintenance to keep up with the times. In his article, "The Computer-in-Education Fiasco," John C. Dvorak remarks that "...network computers will break the financial backs of many school districts if they have to be replaced every few years (as they should be)" (85). Besides, "the technology changes so quickly that by the time the bureaucrats make a decision [on what hardware to purchase] the equipment is obsolete" (Kaplan and Rogers 62).

Computers in schools vary widely in teacher, student, and administrative use. For example, students at Liberty High School in Issaqua, Washington have the opportunity to log on and off the Internet at their convenience, and they have their own electronic mail accounts (Hancock 50). On the other hand, many children have very minimal access to technology. It is true that students with computer access have the advantage of exploring a new and exciting experience; it is also true that children who take family vacations to Africa learn various cultures. But the government is not trying to provide funds for every child in the United States to travel overseas. In effect, although more schools are becoming more technologically advanced, the rate of change for many schools in America is at such a slow pace that, under the current mode of implementation, some will never catch up.

A good teacher-student relationship is vital to the growth of a child. If a student is having trouble in a class, the teacher is there to sense the child's frustration and to help the child to overcome the problem. The computer, however, does not sense emotion, but rather causes the child to be frustrated or bored at redundant or difficult tasks. The point is well stated by Brian Simpson in his article, "Heading for the Ha-Ha":

> Of course, computers can be programmed to do some of the things that teachers do—for example, give information, exercises, and tests—but they cannot deal with unexpected questions or unprogrammed misunderstandings. Human educators—instructors, trainers, tutors—are intuitively

able to do this rather well, but intuition cannot, by definition, be programmed. (86)

So what will happen as a result of the proposed computer revolution? Will the computer replace the teacher at the head of the classroom?

First it was the blackboard, then the overhead projector, and now the computer. The reality exists that most teachers were educated in the Industrial Age with little exposure to computers. In today's Information Age, educators must make extensive efforts to learn the functions of the computers in order to teach the children of this new generation. Consequently, the country is dangling between two ages. According to Kaplan and Rogers, "Teachers will have to get as comfortable with computers as blackboards, or it will be a waste of money" (60). How many teachers will be able to do that?

Contrary to the popular belief that computers are essential to a good education, these allegations are not necessarily true. Educators and administrators are so quick to find ways to integrate computers into mainstream schools that they are overlooking the negative aspects. Are the computer advocates of this country trying to evolve mankind into a digital machine? Although this proposal may seem absurd, is it stretching to say that computer advocates are creating an image where a world community becomes united in thought processes? Cuban is correct to say that "computers can do what they do well, but what they can do well may not be best for students' development, learning, or instruction" (205). All the hype about the Information Age and the vast possibilities for students growing up in this era may be a smokescreen to hide needed educational reforms. When it comes to uniting the traditional classroom environment with technology that educators know so little about, administrators and others are jumping into a swimming pool without first checking to see if there is water in it. Budget plans are being drawn up to fund computers in schools before the long-term effects are considered. If computers take center-stage in classrooms, children may lose the relationships that develop between them and teachers to a rectangular computer monitor. They may also suffer from the lack of social interaction between classmates as a result of this advancing technology. In conclusion, computer advocates need to reexamine the possible harm that the computer revolution can create for students if they are incorporated into traditional classrooms without proper scrutiny and planning. Our children's classrooms should not be experimental laboratories for the new technology; they should use traditional methods until the new methods are proven effective.

WORKS CITED

Clinton, William J. "Executive Order 12999-Ensuring Technology: Ensuring Opportunity for All Children in the Next Century." Weekly Compilation of Presidential Documents. <http://sbweb2.med.iacnet.com/infotrac/session/924/967/20785224/sig!6> (19 March 1997).

Cuban, Larry. "Computers Meet Classroom: Classroom Wins." *Teachers College Record* 95: 185–210.

Cuffaro, Harriet K. "Microcomputers in Education: Why Is Earlier Better?" Sloan 21–30.

Dvorak, John C. "The Computers-in-Education Fiasco." *PCMagazine* <http://sbweb2. med.iacnet.com/infotrac/session/924/967/2078524/7?xrn_1> (19 March 1997).

Hancock, LynNell. "Computer Gap: The Haves and the Have-Nots." *Newsweek* 27 February 1995: 54–4.

Kaplan, David A., and Adam Rogers. "The Silicon Classroom." *Newsweek* <http://sbweb2.med.iacnet.com/infotrac/session/924/967/2078524/sig!5> (19 March 1997).

Simpson, Brian. "Heading For the Ha-Ha." Sloan 84–92.

Sloan, Douglas, ed. *The Computer in Education: A Critical Perspective.* New York: Teachers College Press, 1984.

:-> :-) **T r y T h i s** :-O ;-)

Put It All Together   Now that you have focused and narrowed your topic, found sources both online and offline, and developed a thesis, pull all of this information and insight together and write a research paper similar to Nancy Matthews' paper. You can do this paper either in a traditional, linear mode, or if you wish, see Chapter 5 for information about doing your paper as a hypertext and posting it to the World Wide Web.

Use a *real voice* in this paper. Be yourself, but be your best self: clear, concise, straightforward, and assertive. *Present both sides* of your topic, and be fair when the other side has the stronger argument. Write to a *real audience for a real purpose.*

FIND A JOB ON THE INTERNET

In addition to using the Internet for scholarly research, you can also use it to find information for your own career or your personal life. Many people have found jobs—either temporary, summer jobs or permanent full-time jobs—by using the resources of the Internet to locate job ads or key people at various organizations and businesses. Read the following newspaper story to find out how two university students found summer jobs. After you have read the story, try the job-hunting exercise at the end of the article.

< @ > :- "FINDING WORK VIA INTERNET: :-> :-<
< @ JOB HUNTERS GET A TECHNOLOGICAL LEG UP" -<

*By Laura Gardner, Associated Press (*Wilmington News-Journal, 4/22/95)

L ooking for a job? No need to blacken your fingers on help-wanted ads or chase down busy headhunters. Some of the hottest career resources available today can be found through our home computer.

Job hunters are turning in growing numbers to the Internet and its World Wide Web and subscriber on-line systems for a leg up on the competition. Many of the services offer company profiles, job postings and career counseling.

Some even allow candidates to submit resumes electronically.

"I got a job with a company that never, ever would have put an ad in a newspapers," said Bryan Cantrill, a *Brown University junior* [emphasis added] who used the Internet to land a summer spot at QNX Software Systems Ltd. in Ottawa.

"There's no way I would have found this opportunity—or they would have paid any attention to me—through traditional means."

E-Span Interactive Employment Network, for example, is a free service found on the Internet and accessible through numerous outlets, including CompuServe and America Online. More than 3,500 job postings from 1,700 companies are available at any given time, updated daily and turned over every four weeks.

Career Mosaic offers similar services on the World Wide Web. Sun Microsystems Inc., Tandem Computers Inc, and Intuit Inc., among other technology firms, use Career Mosaic to promote themselves and recruit job applicants.

And while computer and high-tech companies predominate, on-line career forums are by no means the sole preserve of technophiles.

Wisconsin, North Carolina and New York are among a growing number of states and cities that advertise civil service jobs on the Internet. *There are bulletin boards for virtually every profession, including journalism, marketing, theater and the music industry* [emphasis added].

The University of Wisconsin at Madison coordinates Project Connect, which helps place school personnel, trained there or at other universities, in new positions.

"Project Connect puts school districts with job openings in direct contact with teachers and administrators looking for positions," said Steve Head, who oversees the network. "All it takes is an Internet address."

Speed and ease of use inspire many to take their job searches into cyberspace.

Alan Shusterman, a software engineer with Oracle Corp. in Redwood Shores, Calif., relied heavily on e-mail while he was looking for a programmer's position.

"It's so easy," he said. "Click a button and your resume goes out to 30 people—no stamps, no envelopes, no trips to the post office."

Other successful job seekers rave about the access Internet mail afforded them. With electronic mail, applicants can chat with company employees to learn what it's like to work there. Assertive candidates can bypass human resources departments and communicate directly with executives responsible for hiring.

Scott Johnston, a junior at Brown and a roommate of Cantrill, won a summer job on a NASA research team after exchanging electronic messages with the project's director.

"E-mail allowed me to contact someone high up at NASA," he said. "I felt that calling would be an interruption in his day, but e-mail was OK."

Employers also boast of on-line recruiting's benefits. "Overall, it's a more seasoned and more experienced mix of people than I get from a newspaper ad," said Dick Dunkin, recruiting manager for Hal Computer Systems, based in Campbell, Calif. Hal Computer has already hired one applicant through Career Mosaic.

Still, even in high-tech fields some are reluctant to embrace a "paperless" application process.

Terry Williams, a recruiter for technology companies in the Philadelphia and New York areas, complained that electronic resumes frequently appear unformatted on his computer screen, since fonts and margins can differ based on the computer and software used to create the documents.

"I treat an e-mail resume as a fax," he said. The professional way to do things is to follow up with a hard copy."

It works both ways.

Cantrill, who researched companies, circulated his resume, entertained offers and negotiated his salary entirely via the Internet, conceded, "There are some things you want on paper.

Like what?

"Like the final offer," he said with a grin.

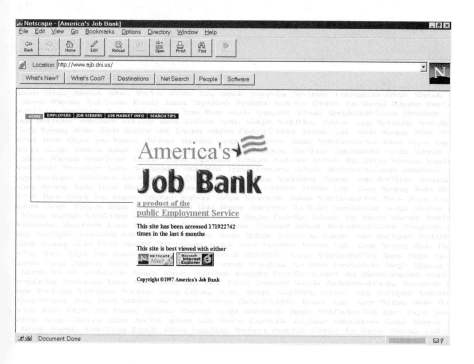

:-> :-) Try This :-O ;-)

Find a Job   Visit one of the job Web sites such as Project Connect (http://careers.soemadison.wisc.edu/httpddoc/pconnect/regform.htm), America's Job Bank (http://www.ajb.dni.us/) or Online Career Center (http://www.occ.com/) and search for a job. Look for a summer job or a long-term job, depending on your preference. Based on your experience researching job opportunities at this site, write a one-paragraph evaluation of its usefulness for students—especially students in your major or with your interests. Post your paragraph on the class e-mail list or distribute it electronically to Usenet groups or list-servs you participate in.

Another way to look for a job is to send e-mail to key people at various organizations or businesses. Like the students at Brown, use the resources of the WWW to look up the e-mail addresses for people who hold key positions at a business or organization you would be interested in joining. You can probably locate a home page for the organization by using AltaVista or one of the other search engines and typing in the name of the organization. Then click on the name of one of the key people to see if you can discover the e-mail address. Send a brief message introducing yourself and your background and enquiring about the possibility of employment. Report your job-hunting experience to the students in your class by posting a note on the class listserv.

PUBLISHING TO THE WORLD

DEVELOPING A WEB SITE: GETTING READY

Many writers are excited about the publishing possibilities on the World Wide Web. For the first time, millions of people can publish to the world. New voices can be heard.

Daily new kinds of communities are established online. Home pages connect people with similar interests and provide information for groups or individuals who in the past would have had a great deal of trouble meeting. If you spend even a few minutes exploring the vast numbers of Web sites, you will soon discover a diversity of viewpoints and opportunities for self-expression unparalleled by any medium in the past.

Now that you have learned to use the Web as a source of information (see Chapter 4), you can explore its power as a place to post your own personal scrapbook and professional portfolio and find others with similar interests. Using links, you can create a home page with many levels of information and meaning. You can use your page to introduce yourself to the world. You can also use it to make meaning out of your academic experience, finding connections that link your course work to the "real world" in ways you may not have thought about before.

But before you begin to use the power of this new medium, you need to think critically about why some home pages are effective and some are not. To develop critical awareness, you should explore some sites and employ commonly used criteria to critique them. As you explore, you will doubtless add some criteria of your own.

After you have explored and refined your own criteria for effective home pages, you will be ready to build your own site and launch it to cyberspace. When you do that, you will be headed out on an adventure. You will expand your horizons beyond the walls of your college or university, and you will open up all sorts of possibilities for learning and for interaction with others. You may be surprised by what comes back to you from cyberspace—especially if you provide a direct e-mail link on your home page:

Job offers, invitations, friends, long-lost relatives, and so forth may find their way to you. You may discover all sorts of connections to communities you never knew you had.

Analyzing Sites: Getting a Feel for Effective Home Pages

To do this exercise, you will need a word processor, access to the Web, and one of the Web browsers such as Netscape or Internet Explorer. If you are unsure how to load a browser or how to use it to access sites on the Web, contact your instructor or the site director for your campus computer center.

As you surf the Web, you will become a sophisticated observer of why some sites attract you and some repel you. If you have a background in visual communication, you may quickly become proficient at understanding why some sites are more effective than others. If you have never thought about visual communication before, you may need to spend some time just looking at the colors and graphics of the Web and becoming aware of how they help (or hinder) the words that appear on the screen.

After you have observed sites critically for a while, you will doubtless develop your own criteria for effectiveness. But in case you are new to site evaluation, here are some hints to help you get started.

Basic Criteria for Evaluating Web Sites

1. What is the purpose of the site? Does it accomplish its purpose?
2. Who is the audience for the site? Does the site fulfill the needs of the audience?
3. Is the site attractive and easy to navigate, or is it cluttered and frustrating? Are colors and graphics distracting or helpful?
4. Is the site easy to find? Does it take too long to load?
5. Does the site provide links to other useful information? Do all the links work?
6. Is the information presented clearly and effectively in small chunks? Is it useful?
7. Does the site fulfill a need that was not met before with print media?
8. Does the site provide addresses, names of contacts to help with community-building?

:-> :-) **Try This** :-O ;-)

Examine Three or More Web Sites

Examine three or more Web sites using the criteria suggested above. Try to find three sites that are comparable: for example, three home pages written by students at your school or at some other college or university; or three pages on a similar topic or theme (for example, see critiques on page 165 under Censorship of two home pages on basketball and two on the Green Movement).

As you compare and contrast these sites, determine which site(s) seem most effective. Why? As you look at sites, refine the suggested list of criteria. Share the results of your exploration with your classmates on the class list-serv or face-to-face.

In addition to critiquing sites on your own, spend some time looking at the sites suggested by your classmates. Work in small groups to critique sites together.

Note: If you are a skilled surfer, you may also want to examine the criteria for Web pages given at The Alliance for Computers and Writing, http://english.ttu.edu/acw/, or Writing for the World by Keith Dorwick, http://www2.uic.edu/~kdorwick/world.html.

Downloading an HTML Editor   If you have access to the WWW, you can use Yahoo!, AltaVista, or other search engines to find free Web editors that you can download. To build a site you will need to use hypertext markup language (HTML). You can type the code yourself (see pp. 138–39 and Appendix D for the code), or you can use an "editor" —a program that converts standard word-processor documents to HTML.

New editors are being created all the time. Each generation makes coding documents for the Web easier. Look around until you find the editor you are most comfortable with.

Note: Although some of these editors even enter the code for you, *it's important that you learn some basic HTML commands so that you can fix things if you wish.*

CREATING A PERSONAL HOME PAGE

After you have evaluated several home pages, you may be ready to construct a personal page of your own. To create an effective page, you need to do some text planning. You also need to learn to think visually. To do an effective Web page, you must be a writer, but you must also be able to visualize the appearance of your page. You need to think about white space and chunks of information, colors, fonts, graphics, and links.

Most writers begin publishing on the Web by creating a home page that introduces them to the world. Usually, these pages have some information about the writer's personal and professional lives. But many home pages sound alike: This is my family; these are my pets; this is my hobby, and so forth. There is an art to creating a page with a voice—one that really represents you to the world. If you want your page to stand out, you should spend some time thinking about what makes you unique.

:-> :-) **Try This** :-O ;-)

Plan Your Personal Home Page   Begin by making a list of your interests and your personality traits. Do you play a musical instrument? Do you like to hike or paint pictures? What courses have you taken? What courses might you take in the future? Do friends describe you as hardworking and intelligent, or friendly and enthusiastic? How would you describe yourself? Trustworthy, loyal, honest, dependable, daring, courageous, risk-taking, innovative? Let your Web page show your most outstanding characteristics.

After you have made a basic list, do some drawing or scribbling to see how your traits link together. For example, if you play a musical instrument and also like to tinker with tools, there may be a connection. Do you find any crossovers or connections between your personal life and your academic life? Do you have any personal philosophy or religious beliefs that seem to bind together both your personal and professional goals? As you find the traits that bind your personality together, you will also discover where to put links in your text.

Design Your Web Page on a Personal Computer   If possible, save your work on the hard drive of a personal computer. When you have finished designing your Web page, you will publish it by uploading it to a server for the Web.

‹ @ › **CREATING A SITE ON THE WWW** :-› :-‹

1. *Do some brainstorming.* Make a list of your activities, hobbies, interests. Try to find the things that make you unique.
2. *Arrange these interests in clusters or categories.* Make a front page or index page that has a menu of links to go to the pages about you.
3. *Open your word processor or an HTML editor and create a file for each of these pages.* Enter the tags for HTML (see list on pp. 138–39). Save each file in the same directory as an ASCII or generic file with the extension *.htm* or *.html.* This removes the coding such as boldface and italics that you applied with your word processor. Use *.htm* if you are working on a PC; use *.html* if you are working on a Mac.
4. *Open your browser.* Open your index file in the browser. View your document. Click on each one of the links to see if it goes to the attached file. If not, go back to the HTML code and fix things.

"Sample Student Home Page," by Harlan Landes   The following Web page by Harlan Landes, a student at the University of Delaware, demonstrates an excellent grasp of how to project a personality with a voice. Although Harlan does provide the usual information about his hobbies, family, and academic pursuits, he also includes his favorite quotations, pictures of his favorite musical groups, and career plans. He does all this with an obvious sense of humor and balance. Harlan clearly demonstrates that he takes himself seriously—but not *too* seriously! When we visit Harlan's home page, we have a sense of really meeting him—getting to know him as a person. That's a good thing to aim for when designing a home page.

WEB PAGES AND SOURCE CODE

All Web pages have an underlying page of HTML editing source code. This is the page on which you actually write the text and insert the commands/tags to create headings, paragraph breaks, add visuals, and so forth.

To understand the difference between the Web page and the underlying HTML editing page, look at Harlan Landes's home page. The underlying source code appears on p. 136. The Web page itself appears below.

Whois

```
<HTML>
<HEAD>
<TITLE> Who is Harlan Landes?</TITLE>
</HEAD>
<BODY   TEXT=#"FFFFFF"   BGCOLOR="OOOOOO"   LINK="OOFFFF"
VLINK="#008080" ALINK="000000" BACKGROUND="harlan.gif">

<CENTER> <P> IMG SRC="harlan.gif"><BR>

<B><FONT   SIZE=+4>Harlan   Luke   Landes</FONT></B></P>
<CENTER>

<CENTER> <P> <FONT SIZE=+1> Hi there.  I'm Harlan.  This is what I
looked like several years ago. I'm waiting to find another picture I can use
instead.  So until then you'll have to deal with looking at this long-haired
freak instead.</FONT></P></CENTER>

<CENTER>   <P>   <A  HREF="back.html"><IMG   SRG="whoback.gif"
ALT="[background]" </A> <BR>
<A HREF="college.html"><IMG  SRC="college.gif" ALT="[college  life]"
</A? <BR>
<A HREF="interests.html"><IMG  SRC="interests.gif" ALT="[interests]"
</A> <BR>
<A  HREF="resume.html"><IMG   SRC="resume.gif"   ALT="[resume]"
</A> </P> </CENTER>
</BODY>
<HTML>
```

Note: Harlan used an ALT tag for readers whose browsers don't support
graphics. If the reader cannot see the picture, she will see the word "background." IMG SRC = image source. This is a .gif file stored in the same directory as Harlan's .html files.

If you want to see what Harlan's page looks like on the Web, point your
browser to: http://www.harbrace.com/english/

:-> :-) **Try This** :-O ;-)

Background Planning for Your Home Page   Following the example of Harlan Landes, do some background planning for your home page. First, look at
your list of interests and personality traits. Establish categories, and think in
terms of chunks of information. You may find you have chunks of academic
stuff, chunks of hobbies or interests, and chunks of favorite things or people.
Remember, readers are not likely to read your home page straight through

from start to finish. They are likely to skip around, clicking on hot words in your hypertext, so each chunk should be intelligible all by itself, but together all of the chunks should make a whole larger than the sum of the parts. Together, the chunks should say: This is me! Lay out your page carefully, perhaps even sketching it on paper. It is important that you see the connectedness of your document before you do any HTML coding.

As you design your page, think in terms of categories or headings. Sketch out each category with a word processor. Mark the words that seem important and consider whether you want to provide a graphic or a link to give the reader a choice to explore these meaningful words or phrases in more depth. Save each file as a generic or ASCII file with the extension *.htm,* on a PC, or *.html* on a Mac. *Put all of the files in the same directory or folder.*

SAMPLE DIRECTORY OR FOLDER WITH .HTM AND .GIF FILES

Filename: homepage.htm

Files:

index.htm

personal.htm

professional.htm

mypicture.gif

SAVING FILES FOR HTML

When you use a word processor to create files for the Web, *you must save the file as plain text or ASCII.* This removes the coding, such as boldface and italics, that you applied with your word processor.

If you are uncertain how to save your document as a plain text file, consult your instructor or the computer lab site assistant. Usually, you go to the File menu, choose Save As, then scroll in the box until you find ASCII or generic.

Your Web pages will work better if you get in the habit of using all lowercase letters and no spaces in file names.

:-> :-) **Try This** :-O ;-)

Paste Up a Paper Version of Your Site   To help you visualize your site, print out your files and do a cut-and-paste version of your Web site similar to Harlan's. To create an effective hypertext, you need to imagine the different paths that readers might take through your document, and you need to think of "logical chunks"—masses of information that fit together in small files that you can link to your home page.

< @ >   :-)   **DANGER: MEMORY HOGS** O :->   :<

When planning a Web page, it's important to consider that while it's fun to add graphics, they are real memory hogs. They slow down the time it takes for a reader to load your site.

As you think about your site, ask yourself, is this graphic necessary? What purpose does it serve? What does it tell about me? Is this graphic just decoration, or does it add real meaning to my message?

Long files of text are also memory hogs because they take a long time to load. Break your information into chunks that load quickly.

Basic HTML   After you have a basic idea of what you want your site to look like, you are ready to start turning your word-processed files into a Web document. To do this, you need to learn some basic HTML (hypertext markup language). **Note:** Although there are several software packages on the market or available free on the Web that will make a page easier to put together, it's still a good idea for you to have a basic idea of how Web documents work because sometimes you may want to change a document written with a software package. If you don't know any HTML code, you won't be able to do so.

To make a basic home page, you really have to know only a few HTML tags. This is a list of the commands you need to start with.

Basic HTML Tags   To change a word-processor file to a hypertext document for the WWW, you need to know the following commands, also known as *tags*:

<HTML>   This tag announces that this is a hypertext document.

<HEAD>   This tag announces that a title or heading will be created.

<TITLE>   These two tags belong around the title at the top of the
</TITLE>   screen.

</HEAD>   This tag closes the heading.

<BODY>   This tag opens the body of your document.

<H1>   This tag indicates the relative size of the headline you wish to use. <H1> is largest; <H6> is much smaller. Each needs an accompanying closing tag such as </H1> or </H6>.

</BODY>   This tag closes the body of your document.

</HTML>   This tag indicates the end of your HTML tags.

CREATE A TEMPLATE

Type the basic HTML tags into your word processor. Save the file as template.htm (on a PC) or template.html (on a Mac). Each time you create a new Web page, retrieve the template file and fill in the blanks.

VIEW THE SOURCE CODE

If you want to see how other Web writers have created their pages, you can view the source code. While looking at an interesting page, select your browser's View Source command and examine how the writer coded the document. You can save the file to your hard drive or a floppy disk if you use the Save As command. Then you can use the code (with your teacher's permission) and substitute your own information. If you want to know how to use a file as a template, ask your teacher for information. See p. 161 for a discussion of the Ethics of Cloning Code.

BACK UP YOUR FILES

When you are preparing files for the WWW, always save a backup version of your work—especially while you are learning how to create HTML documents.

More About HTML   As you may have noticed, HTML tags usually come in pairs—a beginning tag and an ending tag—and are enclosed by angle brackets (< >). The usual form for an HTML tag is

<tag name>Text from your document</tag name>

Notice that the closing tag name is preceded by a slash (/). To turn codes off in your document, you must remember to include the ending tag with the slash in front of it. For example, if you turn on bold and forget to turn it off, the remainder of your document will be bold.

Now you are ready to begin turning a word-processed document into an HTML document so that you can launch it onto the WWW.

< @ >   STEPS TO CREATING A WWW PAGE

1. Using the codes given on pp. 138–39, *insert HTML codes* into each of the minifiles you have created.
2. *Save your word-processor file as a plain text or ASCII file.* If you are not sure how to do this, ask your instructor or a site assistant. In many word processors you choose Save As from the File menu and scroll the box at the bottom of the screen to click on *text file* or *ASCII file.*
3. *Open a browser such as Navigator or Internet Explorer* to see if your text looks as you want it to. With most browsers, you look under the File menu, select Open File or Open Local File, select the name of the file you want to open, and click OK. In some browsers, you may have to type the name of the file in a pop-up window.

:-> :-) **Try This** :-O ;-)

Use the Basics of HTML to Create a Skeleton for Your Home Page   Open your word-processing program. A basic one such as NotePad works well because it automatically saves the file as ASCII text, but if you prefer to work with a brand-name software package such as Microsoft Word or WordPerfect, you will have to remember to save your file as generic type.

After you have opened your word-processor (text editor) program, type the following text:

```
<HTML><HEAD>
<TITLE>
Yourfirstname Yourlastname's Home Page
</TITLE>
```

```
</HEAD>
<BODY>
<H1> Emily Dickinson's Home Page (substitute your name)</H1>
</BODY>
```

Save the file as a plain text or ASCII file. If you are creating the file on a Macintosh computer, call it *index.html.* Otherwise, call it *index.htm.*

You may type HTML commands in either upper- or lowercase letters, or in mixed case. To see the commands more easily, you may want to type them in uppercase. Press Return or Enter at the end of each line.

Now that you have created a bare bones home page, you are ready to add some flesh.

Open a browser such as Navigator or Internet Explorer.

In the browser, select Open File (or the equivalent, depending on the browser you're using) from the File menu.

Select the directory or folder where your HTML file is located, and click OK.

Select the name of the file you wish to open: *index.htm.* Your new home page should appear in the browser window. On some browsers, you may have to type the name of the file in a pop-up window.

When you are ready to add some information to the body of your home page, return to the editor. If you are uncertain how to do this, check with your instructor.

Following is an example of how one writer, Emily Dickinson, a famous poet who lived as a recluse in Amherst, Massachusetts, from 1830 to 1886, might have done a home page about her life and work. During her lifetime, Dickinson published only a dozen poems, but after her death, hundreds of poems were found in her bureau drawers. They were finally published in 1955. Because she was such a private person, the home page done in her memory both reveals and conceals much about her personal life and its relationship to her work. Read the process for her page carefully, and use it as a model to develop your own page. While Emily's page is developing, yours can, too.

Adding Information to the Body of Your Home Page
Now the real fun begins. You can begin to create a page that reflects *you—your* talents, abilities, interests, goals, and passions.

To do this, you need to know a few more basic codes or tags:

Paragraphs <p> and </p>: Use the paragraph codes to indicate where you want a new paragraph to begin. HTML does not pay any attention to regular ways of creating paragraphs. It needs to see the <p> code to begin a paragraph and the </p> code to end one.

Breaks
 or <br>: Use the <br> code to end a short line with no extra spaces between the lines. For example, you might use this code in an address:

Emily Dickinson
Department of English
Amherst College
Amherst, MA 62741

This tag is used alone. There is no </br> tag. It is not used interchangeably with the <p> tag.

Codes for ordered lists <ol>: <ol> creates ordered lists, which number items sequentially. For example, if you want to create a table of contents to list and number the divisions of your home page, you could type

<ol>
<li> My friends and family
<li> My hobbies and interests
<li> My academic pursuits
</ol> (This tag ends the list.)

Unordered lists <ul>: These lists use *bullets* to indicate items. Tags for an unordered list are <ul> and </ul>. If you want your list to use bullets instead of numbers, use the <ul> code at the beginning and the </ul> code at the end.

Adding bold, italics, and underlining: If you want your documents to have some style, you can use simple graphic elements such as bold text (<b> </b>), italics (<I> </I>), or underlining (<u> </u>).

CHECK YOUR O'S AND 0'S AND YOUR L'S AND 1'S.

When writing HTML code, it's important to distinguish between the letter O and the number 0 and the letter l and the number 1. Proofread your code to see if you have used the correct key, or your home page will not work.

:-> :-) Try This :-O ;-)

Add More Text and Formatting to Your Home Page   Let's add <p>, <br>, lists, bold, italics, and underlining to your home page.

Open your *index.htm* file in your word-processing program or text editor and create some paragraphs. Perhaps you want to begin by giving some basic background about yourself and providing a list of important categories that will eventually become links to other in-depth files about yourself.

For example, if Emily Dickinson wanted to add to her home page, she would first open her basic file.

```
<HTML><HEAD>
<TITLE>
Yourfirstname Yourlastname's Home Page
</TITLE>
</HEAD>
<BODY>
<H1> Emily Dickinson's Home Page (substitute your name)</H1>
</BODY>
```

Next, she would move her cursor to the place just after the closing tag for her heading for the body of her home page </H1> and just before the closing tag for the body </BODY>. Then she would begin to type an introductory paragraph about herself.

For example, she might say:

```
<HTML> <HEAD>
<TITLE>
Emily Dickinson's Home Page
</TITLE>
</HEAD>
<BODY>
<H1> Emily Dickinson's Home Page</H1>
<P>
```
Hello. Welcome to my home page. Although I have never traveled much outside of my home town of Amherst, Mass., I am happy to have visitors at a distance and to be able to travel in my imagination to the world of cyberspace.`</P>`

```
<UL>
<li> My Family
<li> Father: "His heart was Pure and Terrible . . ."
<li> Brother Austin and Sister Lavinia
<li> Freshman year at South Hadley Female Seminary
<li> Helen Hunt Jackson: My Friend
<li> Sister Sue: Austin's Wife
<li> Favorite Poems: Letters to the World
<li> Charles Wadsworth: "I am poor once more."
<li> Thomas Wentworth Higginson: Cutting Criticism
<li> Secret Thoughts
</UL>
<p>
```
These are a few of my favorite things: `<b>` Beauty!`</b>` `<I>`Love!`</I>`
`<u>`Nature!`</u>`

Please send e-mail to EDickinson@Amherst.edu.
</BODY>

If Emily looked at her home page now, she would see this:

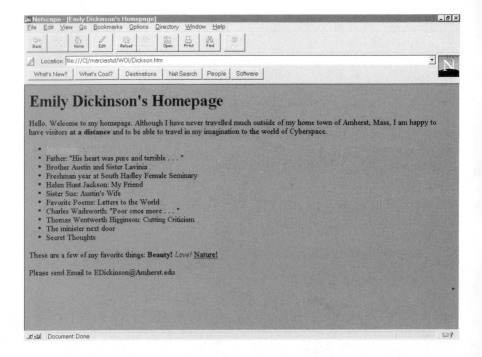

It's a start, but still quite sparse, and there are no links to take readers into her world—only a list of things important to her. But already, we are intrigued—what about her family? What happened her freshman year at South Hadley (later to become Mount Holyoke College) that seemed to drive her away from much contact with outsiders? What about Helen and Sue? What about her poems? Do they reveal any of her Secret Thoughts? So, already we have a sense of Emily's nature—private, introspective, sensitive. And we think we may get a peek into her world.

Now you are ready to create some mystery on *your* home page.

Type an introductory paragraph, using the <p> and </p> codes to start and stop the paragraph. Then create a list that will give readers a hint of what they will find if they stay a while at your home page. (In the next exercise you will add links that will take readers from your list into a now-hidden world of information about you.)

If you wish, add a message at the bottom of the page about sending e-mail to you.

Save this document as a text file or ASCII file. Then return to the browser and reload the page. If you need help doing that, ask the teacher or the site assistant. With some browsers, you go to the Edit menu and choose Reload.

How does the page look to you now? If you want to make some changes in its appearance—if, for example, the list does not appear as a list but as a solid line of text—go to the Edit Document Code choice, often under the Edit menu, and choose to Edit the Code. The program may ask you to specify a word-processing program. Choose the program you are most comfortable with. The advantage of working with a program such as NotePad is that it automatically saves the file in ASCII or a generic format. If you need help moving between your browser and your editor, ask your instructor.

ONLINE HELP FOR CREATING WEB PAGES

Here are some Web addresses that can help you learn how to put information on the World Wide Web. They are provided by the World Wide Web Consortium. For advanced style guides, see Appendix D.

http://222.23.org/pub/WWW/Provider/Overview.html

"A Beginner's Guide to HTML"

http://www.nesa.uiuc.edu/General/Internet/WWW/HTML/Primer.html

"How Do They Do That with HTML?"

http://www.nashville.net/~carl/htmlguide/index.html.

Adding Links Within the Document and to Other Documents Now Emily adds *links* to her secret files so that we begin to see her more fully.

Emily has prepared a list of impressions and information about her family—especially her father, who was a dominant force in her life. She also has information and impressions about her first year in college; her friend, Helen Hunt Jackson; her sister-in-law, Sister Sue; her favorite poems, which lay hidden in a trunk for many years before their discovery; her admirer, Charles Wadsworth; her most serious critic, T. W. Higginson; and her Secret Thoughts (she used capital letters to indicate their importance).

Now she is ready to add hypertextual links to the bulleted list in her document so that when readers click on one of the items in her list, they can go behind the screen to peek at some of her "hidden" thoughts.

Emily goes back to the code for her document. She has already prepared chunks of information and impressions in separate files for each of the items on her list and saved each chunk as a separate file in the same directory with her home page. She gave each of the files the extension *.htm* (or *.html* if she used a Macintosh) and entered tags for headings, lists, and so forth.

SOURCE FOR EMILY DICKINSON'S HOME PAGE

Much of the information for Emily Dickinson's home page can be found at http://www.planet.net/pkrisxle/emily/dickinson.html.

Her letters to Higginson and others can also be found at this site. If Emily wanted to create a link to this site from her home page, she would just type *<A HREF= "http://www.planet.net/pkrisxle/emily/dickinson.html">Letters </A >*within her code. Then a hot link would appear on the screen when she looked at her page with the browser. The reader could click on the link and go to the site with her letters.

To make the information appear when readers clicked on one of the items on her home page, she had to use *anchor tags* (<A HREF=>), which she embedded in the code of her document.

Anchor tags look like this:

<A HREF=filename.htm>Name of the item
that is the "hot word" in your document</A>

For example, Emily wanted to add a file called *family.htm* that would create a link for the item *My Family* in her bulleted list. In the code for her document, she found the words *My Family* and typed the anchor code around them. Here's how the code looked when she added the link in her *index.htm* document to the *family.htm* file—the file that holds her thoughts and impressions about her family:

```
Emily Dickinson's Home Page
</TITLE>
</HEAD>
<BODY>
<H1> Emily Dickinson's Home Page</H1>
<P>
Hello. Welcome to my home page. Although I have never traveled much out-
side of my home town of Amherst, Mass., I am happy to have visitors at a
distance and to be able to travel in my imagination to the world of cyber-
space.</P>

<UL>
<li><A HREF=family.htm> My Family</A> (This is the added code.)
<li> Father: "His heart was Pure and Terrible . . ."
<li> Brother Austin and Sister Lavinia
<li> Freshman year at South Hadley Female Seminary
<li> Helen Hunt Jackson: My Friend
<li> Sister Sue: Austin's Wife
```

```
<li> Favorite Poems: Letters to the World
<li> Charles Wadsworth: "I am poor once more."
<li> Thomas Wentworth Higginson: Cutting Criticism
<li> Secret Thoughts
</UL>

<p>
These are a few of my favorite things: <b> Beauty!</b>  <I>Love!</I>
<u>Nature!</u>
Please send e-mail to EDickinson@Amherst.edu.
</BODY>
```

Following is what Emily's file *family.htm* looks like. Notice that she has set up the page just like her home page with the same heading at the top, but the information in the body section of the page is much different. This is the information that will appear if a reader clicks on the hot words *My Family* on Emily's home page. This time, instead of creating a bulleted list on various topics, she gives an impression of her family. Of course, she could have gone into much more detail, creating links from this page to separate pages about family members such as her grandfather, for example. But she chose not to. You may make a different choice for your page.

```
<HTML><HEAD>
<TITLE>
Emily Dickinson's Home Page
</TITLE>
</HEAD>
<BODY>
<H2> My Family</H2>
```

My family has a tradition of excellence, and sometimes it is hard for me to live up to it.
My grandfather was one of the founders of Amherst College, and my father is the treasurer.
My brother, Austin, is weak and ineffectual, so I feel really pressured to succeed.
My sister, Lavinia, always wants to take care of me. I wish she would stop!
On the other hand, I don't want to spend my life doing all the things women do—taking care of sick people and the elderly.
I really do want to spend my time writing.
```
</BODY></HTML>
```

:-> :-) **Try This** :-O ;-)

Expand the Information for *Your* Home Page   If you created a bulleted list on your home page, now turn that list into *hot words* that will trigger a hypertext and create the files to attach to that list. To create a real impression for your readers, don't just give facts; instead, aim for a mood and a tone. Do you want your page to be upbeat and lively? Then use language and links that have lots of positive energy. Do you want your page to be thoughtful and insightful? Then your language should reflect that spirit.

First, create the files you will attach, chunking information in short files, usually no more than one or two screens long, and save each file with the extension *.htm* or *.html.* Set up each file with the usual template <HTML> <HEAD><TITLE> and so forth. See the instructions above if you need a refresher. Remember, save the file as a text file or generic word-processing file.

When you finish writing the short information files, go back to the code for your home page and add the links, using the format *<A HREF= "filename.htm"> Name of the item in your list that you want to turn into a hot word </A>.* If you want to link to a site on the WWW, type the URL in the space for filename. Provide context for a link. Use short phrases that clearly describe the link and what readers will find if they choose to follow it. Readers don't like to be completely in the dark when they choose a link. For example, don't just say, "Click Here."

Try it now. If you get stuck, look back at the example of the code for Emily Dickinson's Home Page on p. 146.

< @ >   : -)   PROOFREAD WEB PAGES   ○   ; - >   : <

Many Web pages look sloppy because they are filled with spelling and punctuation errors. Don't let yours be one of them.

Run a spell checker on your text and look carefully at your grammar and punctuation. Remember, this page will represent you to millions of readers in cyberspace, and you don't want sloppy errors to spoil the impression.

Adding Color and Graphics   After you get the content established for your home page, it's time to think about adding some finishing touches. Color and graphics can give your page zest. But be careful! Many Web pages have been spoiled by the addition of too many graphics, and some pages are impossible to read because of the colors chosen for the background or the fonts.

When adding color and graphics, go slowly. Save multiple versions of your file so that you can compare the effects and ask others for their opinions. And provide a context for your graphics. Readers should be able to clearly see why you have used a graphic. It should not just be sitting on the page with no apparent reason for being there.

USING GRAPHICS FROM THE WEB

Before using any graphics or text from a Web site on your home pages, ask permission of the owner of the Web page.

Most authors will grant permission if the material will be used for educational, not commercial, purposes. You can usually get permission by writing e-mail to the author of the site.

Graphics and text are copyrighted.

Follow Emily Dickinson's process as she adds graphics to her home page:

Emily decided to add some color and graphics to her page, but first she had to do some planning. She went upstairs to the old family trunk and found pictures of her family—especially one of her father looking tyrannical. She also found some poems in her own handwriting that she wanted to appear on the screen just the way they looked on the paper. In with the poems, she found pictures of Mr. Wadsworth and Mr. Higginson. She used a scanner to digitize her materials so that she could save them on her disk. She knew that Web pages do best with .*gif* files, so when the scanner asked her what format she wished to save the files in, she chose .gif. She was careful to save the graphics files in the same directory as her Web page and her links.

After Emily had all of her files saved, she went back to the code for her home page and entered the HTML code for the graphics in the place where she wanted them to appear. For example, she placed the picture of her father at the top of the page about her family. Since he always seemed larger than life, she used her HTML editor to resize the graphic to make it look so large that it dominated the words.

This is what the code looked like in Emily's file: <H2><img src= "father.gif"> My Family</H2>. She proceeded to do the same thing for each of her graphics, positioning her cursor where she wanted the graphic to appear and typing the code *<img src="name of the graphic file.gif">*. She saved her file, then she opened her browser and reloaded the file to have a look at it. She liked what she saw! The familiar faces added a sort of Victorian portrait gallery to her text; the members of her family looked stiff and forbidding, and the men in her life, Mr. Wadsworth and Mr. Higginson, looked positively distinguished.

Next, she added a color background. To do this, she consulted an online manual with some HTML code for colors. She found that she could choose a background color, a color for the regular text, a color for unvisited links (links the reader hasn't looked at yet), a color for visited links (links the reader has looked at), and a color for the currently active link (the link the reader is looking at currently). For the sake of simplicity, she decided to use color only in the background of her document and to leave the text and link colors set to the way they were. She knew that too many colors in a document can be distracting. **Note:** In his home page, Harlan Landes used color for visited and unvisited links. See p. 136.

Emily found a list of codes for colors at http://www.infi.net/wwwimages/colorindex.html. She copied the following list of basic colors into a file for her use. She noticed that each color was preceded by a # (pound) sign and composed of a combination of numbers and letters.

BASIC HTML COLOR CODES

White	#FFFFFF
Red	#FF0000
Green	#00FF00
Blue	#0000FF
Magenta	#FF00FF
Cyan	#00FFFF
Yellow	#FFFF00
Black	#000000

To insert green as the background color in her document, she used the command <BGCOLOR=#"00FF00"> She typed this command just after the command <BODY and before the closing >. For example, <BODY BGCOLOR:#"00FF00">

:-> :-) Try This :-O ;-)

Add Graphics to Your Home Page   Gather some graphics to add to your home page to give it some personality. If you are skilled as an artist, or if you know how to use a draw and paint software program, you can create some images of your own. Then use a scanner to digitize these graphics. Save them as .gif files on your disk and put them in the same directory as your source code for your Web page.

In your browser, retrieve your home page and choose to edit the source code. (If you need help with this step, ask your instructor or the site assistant.) When you have the source code in front of you, add links to your graphics. To add a link, place the cursor where you want to add the image. Then type <img src="nameofyourfile.gif">. To see how the image looks on your page, save the code file and go to the File menu to choose Browse Document (or the equivalent).

Note: You can also add code to position the image in various places (top of text, center of page, and so forth). For detailed instructions on positioning graphics on a page, consult an online or offline guide to HTML.

When you finish adding your graphics to your document, *try experimenting with background color.* Go back to the source code for your home page. Find the place near the beginning of your document where you have used the <BODY> command. Type a color code in the <>s. For example, if you want your page to be blue, type <BODY BGCOLOR="#0000FF">. Save the file and go to the browser to take a look at your page. If you wish to change the color of the text or to use a more subtle shade of color, consult a guide to HTML.

FORMAT FOLLIES

Don't waste lots of time getting the fonts and colors to appear exactly the way you want them. They will look different to readers using different monitors or browsers. For example, browsers can be set to view fonts in a particular way.

Publish Your Home Page   When you have finished drafting and revising your home page and viewing it with a browser, testing all of the links to see if they work, you are ready to put it on the World Wide Web. To do this, you should contact your instructor or the computer lab coordinator, since the publishing process varies from one location to another.

Try This

Look at Your Page with Several Browsers   If possible, use several browsers, such as Navigator or Internet Explorer or Lynx (text only), to see how it will look to different readers. Test all of the links to make sure that they work. Is it easy to navigate in your document? Show your page to some of your classmates. Ask them for suggestions. For example, it should be easy to return to your first page (usually the Index page) at any time in your document. Revise your page for publication. Then consult your instructor or the computer coordinator for your campus for help uploading your page to the World Wide Web.

Finishing Touches

1. *Date and sign your Web page on the bottom of the first page.*
2. *Link your page to another document on the server of your college or university.* For help with this, ask your instructor.

3. *Add a copyright statement.*
4. *Add the URL (uniform resource locator) of the document for readers who print it out.*
5. *Make sure your e-mail address is correct.*
6. *Check your spelling and grammar.*
7. *Be aware of your personal safety.* Don't publish your home address or phone number, for example.
8. *Remember, even your grandmother can see your page on the Web.* Be sure it represents you as you would like to be seen to the world.

CREATING AN ACADEMIC PORTFOLIO

Now that you have created a personal home page, you can begin to get ready to put your academic portfolio online. To do this, you need to think about several things.

Information vs. Propaganda   Because the Web is so seductive visually and so lively in its texts, it's easy for essays to become supercharged—full of information and links to "sexy" materials, but very low on thoughtful analysis and argumentation. Before writing an academic essay for the Web, you should practice distinguishing between online propaganda—glitzy sites that offer much opinion or information and little thought—and in-depth sites that offer full analysis of the information presented and present both sides of the argument of a controversial issue.

:-> :-) Try This :-O ;-)

Visit Some Sites That Offer Student Essays   You can find student essays at the following sites:

"Writing for the World" by Keith Dorwick
http://www2.uic.edu/~kdorwick/world.html/

Student Projects site at the University of Texas
http://www.cwrl.utexas.edu/studentprojects/index.html/

Choose three essays to critique on the same or similar subjects. Following are some guidelines to help you look at the essays. Perhaps you will want to add other criteria to the list. This exercise can be done in a small group if you wish. All evaluators should critique the same sites and compare their reactions. After the group discusses the sites visited, try to establish criteria that describe an effective academic online essay.

@EVALUATING ACADEMIC ESSAYS ON THE WWW

What is the subject of the online essay?

What is its purpose?

Who is the audience (specifically)?

Is the essay laid out clearly and logically?

Do the links make sense?

Are both sides of an argument presented?

Do the graphics add to the meaning, or do they distract readers from the text?

Are the chunks of text unified, coherent, and developed? Or are they superficial and disjointed?

What is the best feature of this e-text?

How might it be improved?

Defining Audience, Subject, Purpose, and Style   From your observation of the three student-written hypertext essays, you can begin to have a sense of audience, subject, purpose, and style on the WWW and how they are related to one another. If you are going to write effective academic essays online, you need to think about each of these issues before you begin writing. You need to plan.

:-> :-) **Try This** :-O ;-)

Plan an Academic Hypertext   First, choose a subject. If you wish, you can choose an essay you have already written and adapt it for the Web. If you prefer to start with a new essay, do some brainstorming or list making to help you define a subject and focus that subject into a topic for an essay.

For example, one student, Bryan Jariwala, was interested in writing about how writing on the Internet differs from writing on paper. To plan his essay, he did some list making. His list looked like this:

Writing on the Net	Writing on Paper
Hard? Why?	Easy
Many audiences	One specific audience

Purpose is fluid	Purpose is definite
Hidden stuff	Out in the open
Visual and verbal	Verbal
Dynamic	Fixed
Connected	Isolated

Information vs. Analysis   Next, Bryan went searching for some source material for his paper. At the University of Texas site he found some student papers to critique. He had some general opinions about effectiveness, but he decided he needed to read some hypertext theory in order to be able to make informed judgments about the hypertexts. So he read a rough draft of Jay David Bolter's essay "Degrees of Freedom" (http://www.lcc.gatech.edu/faculty/bolter/degrees.html) that argues that writing in cyberspace will lead to a new definition of the "authorial voice": "In cyberspace the self is no longer constructed as an autonomous, authorial voice; it becomes instead a wandering eye that occupies various perspectives one after another." Bolter also argues that because of the computer revolution, "we are witnessing the emergence of a culture in which the preferred mode of representation is visual rather than linguistic and in which the highest value is the ability to assume multiple and unobstructed points of view." Intrigued by these ideas, Bryan decided to try to apply them to the student essays.

After reading Bolter, Bryan also found an another online source: "A Conversation on Information: An Interview with Umberto Eco," by Patrick Coppock (http://www.cudenver.edu/~mryder/itc_data/eco/intro.html). He extracted a quotation from Coppock in which he asks Eco if he has "looked at any of these hyper-books, like those of Jay Bolter and Michael Joyce?" Eco replies, "At the present state of technology, these lenses are very rudimentary, so I don't think that they can really help me to see something more." Bryan found this stimulating.

Bryan then generated a list of criteria by which to judge the essays:

Does the title catch the eye?

Is there too much information presented at once?

Is it too wordy, or is it short and concise?

Does the author use all possible resources [visual and verbal] to strengthen his/her point?

Does it include pictures and/or designs?

If so, are they placed strategically or ineffectively?

Is there effective use of links and hypertext, or do the links confuse the reader?

IMAGES AND ARGUMENT

Caution! In an academic paper, images do not make an argument all by themselves. If you use images, be sure to explicate your argument with words.

Bryan decided that the chief challenge for a Web writer is to keep the reader from clicking to a link elsewhere.

He looked at two student essays from the site at the University of Texas at Austin: "Native American Reservations," by McLain Hall, and "The Toxic Mine Drainage Problem," by Matthew Ruff, and applied his criteria for evaluation. Then he was ready to pull together his research materials and his comments on the essays. He generated an index menu for the "chunks" in his essay which he called "A Look at Web Pages: A Critique of Different Pages," by Bryan Jariwala. The menu looked like this:

The Assignment

Background

The Criteria

The First Analysis

The Second Analysis

The Conclusion

Works Cited

Finally, Bryan pulled it all together. Using HTML, he created minifiles of chunks, stored them in one directory, created the links to his title page, and then to his personal home page, and posted the paper to the Web.

Here is what it looks like:

```
<HTML>
<HEAD>
<TITLE>Research Paper—A Look At Web Pages</TITLE>
</HEAD>
<BODY BGCOLOR="408080" TEXT="000000" LINK="80FF00" VLINK=
"FF80FF" ALINK="000000">
```
Note: Bryan assigned colors for the text, and the links: "visited" (VLINK), "unvisited" (LINK), and "active" (ALINK).

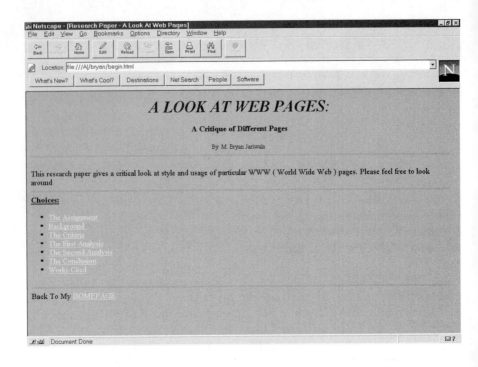

```
<center>
<H1><B><I>A LOOK AT WEB PAGES:</I></B></H1>
A Critique of Different Pages</B><BR>
<BR>
<Font size="-1">By: M. Bryan Jariwala</FONT>
</center>

<HR>
<BR>
<P>This research paper gives a critical look at style and usage of particular
WWW (World Wide Web) pages. Please feel free to look around <BR>
<HR>

<B><U>Choices:</U></B>
<UL>
<LI><A Href="assign.html">The Assignment </A>
<LI><A Href="background.html">Background </A>
<LI><A Href="criteria.html">The Criteria</A>
<LI><A Href="first.html">The First Analysis</A>
<LI><A Href="second.html">The Second Analysis</A>
<LI><A Href="conclusion.html">The Conclusion</A>
<LI><A Href="cited.html">Works Cited</A>
</UL>
```

```
<HR>
Back To My  <A Href="http://me.udel.edu/~jariwamb">HOMEPAGE</A>

</BODY>
</HTML>
```

:-> :-) Try This :-O ;-)

Critique Bryan's Essay   Using Bryan's essay, generate a list of guidelines for effective academic arguments online. To help you look for items, here are some general comments to get you started. Bryan has made a brave beginning into uncharted territory: writing an academic hypertext. I am grateful to him for allowing me to use his work as an example. It has many strengths but also enough problems to be a helpful example, I think.

Be sure to visit Bryan's essay at http://www.harbrace.com/english. To get you started thinking about Bryan's academic hypertext, here are some observations:

1. *Display.* Bryan uses a black background with blue letters; this was very hard to read on my monitor. He pointed out that it was easy to read on his monitor, but when writing for the Web, you should try to keep the background fairly neutral, because different monitors display text differently.

2. *Back arrow.* He forgot to include a way for readers to get back to his title page easily. Therefore, you had to use the Back arrow repeatedly instead of being able to jump directly to the main menu.

3. *Missing documentation.* Bryan gives no documentation for the quote? paraphrase? summary? from Michael Joyce: "Degrees of Freedom." As in a print media research paper, he needs to provide page numbers, publisher, date, and so forth—both in the text itself and in the Works Cited. He also needs to demonstrate mastery of the source material. He should not just paste it into the paper by creating a link to the site.

4. *Web trap.* His critique of the students' papers is the strongest part of his hypertext. He is right on the money when he says, of Hall, that there is "not enough info to explain anything." Basically, Hall's paper falls into the same trap that Bryan's falls into: too much emphasis on the Web, not enough on the content of the paper.

5. *Following through.* In my office, Bryan had raised an interesting issue that he does not go into in his paper: the "scatter effect" of reading and writing online. He does not talk about why it is so difficult to make/read an in-depth argument in hypertext. What about the "chunk effect"?

6. *Proofreading.* For the most part, Bryan has proofread well, but he tends to confuse *too* and *to* and *loose* and *lose*. When we publish to the world, it's especially important to *proofread carefully*.

7. *Conclusion.* His conclusion has a good link to Coppock. It might have been a good idea to quote Eco, too, since he is famous in the field of rhetoric, and since Coppock asked him the question. Eco's response is "right on" in many ways.
8. *Bad Back.* At the end of the link to Coppock, *Back* doesn't take the reader back to Bryan's paper, but to Joyce. It should go back to Bryan.
9. *How to make it work.* His summing-up statement in the conclusion, while thought-provoking, illustrates the lack of development and definition in his own essay. He says, "In order for a paper to be good, it should be able to stop a reader from clicking onwards." But he never says how a reader is "stopped." Does glitz do it, or does the paper need substance to hold a reader?

Now, based on your observation of Bryan's paper (and other academic hypertexts you may have visited at the collections of students' papers), generate a list of criteria for an effective academic hypertext. Your list should address both form and content. This exercise can be done in small groups, if you wish. Post your list to the class listserv. Compare lists to see if you agree or disagree with your classmates.

< @ > DEVELOPING IDEAS IN A HYPERTEXT > :-<

In an academic hypertext, develop important ideas at the beginning of your paper, probably on the first page, or repeat them throughout the text.

Remember, unlike a traditional linear essay, hypertexts are often read randomly. Readers may start at any point, so important ideas need to get early emphasis and repetition.

Synthesizing Sources vs. Pasting Links   Many online academic papers simply create links to sources of information rather than synthesizing the sources and using them to create an argument. An effective online academic writer uses sources not to avoid thought by just linking things together, but rather as a way to *reinforce* thought.

In the past, when you wrote a traditional research paper, you used quotes, paraphrases, and summaries of information from your sources. Now, using hypertext, you will be able to include (in some cases) links to all or many of the sources (see copyright issues, p. 161). In a sense, you will be able to invite your readers to look over your shoulder as you go through the process of examining source material, choosing parts to quote, summarize, or paraphrase. You will be able to share with readers your path to ideas and insights in a way never possible before hypertext. You can even invite readers to interact with your paper: send you e-mail, for example, so that your paper will continue to live after it is published online.

In the past, when you handed a paper to a teacher, you may have wondered if it was worth all of the effort of creation. You knew that once the teacher graded the paper, it was usually dead. It sat in a drawer somewhere until it moved to a wastebasket. But if you publish your essays online and invite others to send you responses by adding your e-mail address to the document along with the HTML code to create an instant e-mail response, your ideas can nourish you and others long after they are written. The dialogue can continue, and your ideas can deepen and mature.

:-> :-) **Try This** :-O ;-)

Critique Some Links   Look at three or more online academic papers from the collections of students' essays and evaluate the writers' use of source materials. (See list of URLs for sources for hypertext research papers on p. 152.) Do they just link source material to their text, or do they comment on the source materials, evaluating them and using them to reinforce and enrich their arguments?

Works Cited can be a good place to provide a direct link to the source, but in your own essay, you should strive to analyze and synthesize, not just paste in whole texts.

Hypertext vs. Linear Writing   Hypertexts differ from linear writing in many important ways—both in form and content. For example, on paper, writers need to think about unity, coherence, and transitions. On the screen, writers need to think about these same three issues, but in different ways—verbally *and* visually. Instead of using transition words, for example, writers need to think about links and what they do to hold a work together. Instead of thinking only about verbal aspects of unity and coherence, Web writers also need to think about visual aspects. How should a page "look"? Does it make a difference if one "page" of the paper has a green background, for example, and the next page has a pink background? What does this do to unity and coherence? Does it matter if all headers at the top of the screen look alike? Why, or why not?

:-> :-) **Try This** :-O ;-)

Critique Use of Source Material   Either singly or in small groups, examine several academic hypertexts. In your estimation, which writer has done the best job of using sources to advance an argument? Which writer has merely created links without analysis or commentary?

REVISING FOR THE WEB

To understand the difference between writing for paper and writing for the Web, take a paper you have already written in a traditional format and revise it as a hypertext. So that you can get started thinking about the process, here are some suggestions.

:-> :-) Try This :-O ;-)

Hypertext One of Your Linear Essays   Choose an essay you have already written for this course or for some other course and revise your essay for the WWW. Keep notes as you go along. When you have finished, share your process with other students on the class listserv. Compare your process and your product with others. How are they similar, how are they different? What have your learned from this process? What will you do differently next time?

<@> :-) POLISH YOUR PAGE ;-O :-> :-<

1. *To give your page a polished look, use a title tag at the top that tells the subject matter of your essay.* Remember, search engines such as Yahoo!, AltaVista, and Excite! use the title tags to index documents.
2. *Include a "last-updated" line in your text.* That way, readers can see if they are reading an old document or one that is still "under construction."
3. *Provide a signature block containing contact and copyright information at the bottom of the main pages.*
4. *Put your essay in a context.* For example, you might link it to other essays you have written (or that others have written) on the same subject, or you might link it to your personal home page.
5. *Remember that some readers will be using a browser such as Lynx that does not support graphics.* Therefore, when you include a graphic in your document, you should give a brief description of it.

Register Your Page   After you have published your page on the Web, send a message to one of the search engines to register your page so that readers can find it when they are searching for information.

URLs to register pages:

http://www.mckinley.com/feature.cgi?.add_bd

http://add.yahoo.com/bin/add?

The Ethics of Cloning   After you experiment with your browser a bit, you will notice that it is possible to view the source code for any page on the Web. It is also possible to copy the code and use it as a template for your own page. But not all Web writers agree about the ethics of this kind of cloning. Some writers feel that the code is there to be shared. Others do not.

:-> :-) **Try This** :-O ;-)

Debate the Ethics of Cloning Web Pages   Have a debate online or face-to-face with others in your class about the ethics of cloning the source code for a home page. Now that you have created a personal page and an academic hypertext (which you may have linked to your personal home page), you have a real stake in this debate. Your page could be cloned! How would you feel about that?

Copyright Issues   Ownership of materials on the Web has been debated a great deal in public and in the courts. To be safe, do not copy graphics or text without written permission from the copyright holder. Of course, you can create links to texts or graphics at other sites, but clearly credit the person who created the graphic or the text. For the most recent information about copyright on the Web, use one of the search engines and search for *copyright*.

:-> :-) **Try This** :-O ;-)

Look for Copyright Violations   Search the Web for sites on a popular topic such as sports or rock music. Which sites seem to abide by copyright law? Which sites seem to violate it? In a small group of classmates, debate the importance of copyright law. Why is it important to protect images and graphics on the Web from plagiarism? What may happen to creativity on the Web if artists and writers do not have protection from theft? Share your thoughts with the class on the class listserv.

Writers and Readers Redefined   In the past, readers and writers hardly ever had a chance to interact. Once a book or an article was published, seldom did readers get a chance to ask writers questions or to contribute ideas for future revisions. Now, publishing on the Web makes all this not only possible, but also probable. This is a revolutionary change, and it bears watching and thinking about.

:-> :-) **Try This** :-O ;-)

Write Comments to Authors   Visit several Web sites and use the e-mail to the author link to comment on the site or to ask questions. Keep a record of your queries and of the responses you receive. Ask the authors if they have received many messages and if the messages have influenced the author's thinking about the site. Share your responses in a small group or on the class listserv.

If you want to know how many readers are visiting your site, add a counter to your home page. See the instructions at http://www.udel.edu/topics/internet/WWWcounter-howto.html.

If you want to get feedback from readers, include a clickable e-mail address. To add instant e-mail possibilities to your page, type: <A HREF= "mailto:youremailname@youremailadress"> Your Name</A>. Save your file as an ASCII file and look at it in your browser. Readers should see *Your Name* as a hot link. If they click on *Your Name*, they should go to a place to write e-mail.

:-> :-) **Try This** :-O ;-)

Add a Counter and an E-mail Link   Add a counter and your e-mail address to your home page. Check the results in your browser. **Note:** You can make the counter secret if you wish. Check with an HTML manual to discover how to add a counter that only you will see.

Style on the Web   In general, keep Web pages simple. If you use too many large graphics and fancy fonts and sounds, your files will take too long to load, and readers will learn to bypass your site.

Your pages will be effective if they are attractive, lead easily to related information, and have a voice. The voice, however, should not be too idiosyncratic, because readers can get a long-lasting impression of you that you might not want them to have. If, for example, you use blinking red dots on a yellow background, that may be okay if your audience is students and your purpose to entertain. But if you are writing to a wider audience, aim for a public persona. Create pages that mirror the kind of impression you might want to make if you were meeting your audience for the first time at a public gathering. In fact, that's a really good analogy, because encountering pages on the Web is a lot like meeting people at a conference, workshop, or party.

First impressions do matter, and if there is little substance, visitors move on with their feet or their mouse.

:-> :-) **Try This** :-O ;-)

Critique Pages for Style   Look carefully at three or more Web pages for both form and content. Here are some criteria to help you get started:

What is the subject of the site? What is the purpose? Who is the audience?

Use of color and visuals: Are they distracting or engaging? Are the colors and visuals well suited to the subject, purpose, and audience of the site? Why or why not?

Use of links: Do the links seem logical and useful? Do they work?

Unity, coherence: Do the various pages of the site seem to fit together visually and verbally to form a whole?

Chunks: Does each page seem like a unified element of its own, while still part of the whole?

Language and tone: Does the language used seem appropriate to the subject, purpose, and audience? Is it highly technical? Is it offensive? Is it too informal for a public space such as the Web?

PRINT VS. ONLINE WRITING

In the following essay, Andrea Schenk argues that the WWW is superior to print sources when it comes to information about her favorite sport—basketball. Read her essay and critique her analysis. Has she defended her position well? Has she overlooked any areas of comparison that she should have considered? Access issues? What do you think of her idea of a hierarchy for sites? What about a review panel rating sites? Share your opinion of Andrea's essay with your classmates.

< @ > "WELCOME TO THE WORLD WIDE WEB!" :-<

By Andrea Schenk

The WWW is quickly filling up with vast numbers of home pages used for many purposes. Some people use them for personal reasons, while others use them for organizations and companies. Web pages are a quick and easy way to find out information about different topics from many different perspectives. I particularly enjoy Web pages about basketball—a very interesting topic to me. While comparing two very different home pages on this topic, I fund some intriguing information and opinions.

First was the National Basketball Association's home page. This was a very fascinating one and very easy to find; with a little common sense, anyone looking for information about basketball while "surfing the web" could just think *NBA* and then type http://www.nba.com in the space for the address. Once surfers arrive at their destination, they find the site extremely user-friendly because it portrays pictures you can click on to extract information about a certain topic. Also, it is concise and factual. Since it is an official publication of the NBA, it has no prejudices or biases. It serves the purpose of allowing people to obtain information on any basketball team, player, or support personnel. Because it can be updated frequently, the information is always current.

There is only really one disadvantage to the page—the fact that users cannot actively interact with people. The page does not provide surfers with a way to contact NBA officials, team members or teams with any questions or concerns they may have. This is unfortunate because if there had a been a way to do this, it would be an even more effective page. But the NBA page is appealing to the eye, and that is one of the most important aspect of home pages. This site definitely fulfills a need that had not been filled before by print media. It is extremely efficient.

There are many sites on the WWW about basketball. Another one is called "Hoopheads" (http://arganet.tenagra.com/~ccarter/hoopheads/yawn/yawn.html). This page, because it is run by an individual, has certain biases and prejudices towards certain teams. It is certainly not as visually sophisticated as the NBA's page, but it is somewhat interactive in that it allows viewers to write comments. The only problem is that if anyone has certain questions about the NBA, the person who made the page may not be able to effectively answer the question. Another problem with this page, and all others like it, is that it is not necessarily factual or informational; therefore, surfers must approach it carefully, because it is not clear who the author is and what his or her biases are.

Many people feel that there are too many home pages on the Internet. But, in order for surfers to get the whole picture, there must be many different types of pages on all the different topics. The Internet is like a puzzle: all of its pieces together equal the whole picture. Without one of the pieces, the picture is not whole. It is possible that one day the Net may be filled to capacity, but what if there were a hierarchy of home pages? Once could place different aspects of a certain topic in order of importance. For example, in the area of basketball, the hierarchy could begin at the general level such as the NBA. Then, the hierarchy could move on to the team, its players, officials, and finally, individual pages with certain clear biases. This idea may help the problem of overcrowding on the Net. There could also be certain officials who can screen every home page and make sure it is suitable and informational. But this would prove to be time consuming and boring; also, it might interfere with the First Amendment and freedom of speech.

In modern day society, the Internet has become a large part of everyday lives. Unfortunately, it is becoming over-crowded and chaotic. But there really isn't anything that can be done to control the proliferation of pages other than screening them, or placing them into a certain hierarchy. Each page has its own uniqueness, and without such diversity, the WWW might become boring and mundane. Surfers must learn from experience to tell the good waves from the bad ones. We will learn much about discriminating fact from opinion and information from propaganda while we navigate the waves.

:-> :-) **T r y T h i s** :-O ;-)

Join the Debate on Web Censorship   In the following essays, two students look at censorship of the Web from different points of view and arrive at different conclusions. Read both essays and evaluate the arguments. Do you agree with Heather that the Web should be censored? Or do you agree with Kyle that it must remain free to all kinds of ideas?

When you have finished evaluating the student essays, write a hypertext essay and post it on your home page arguing for or against censorship of the Web. Add links to sites on the Web to support your argument.

< @ > :-) **"HAVE WE GONE TOO FAR?"** :-> :-<

By Heather D'Agostino

The WWW is quickly filling up with vast number of home pages, and many of them give people the wrong impression of reality. For example, recently I surfed through several pages that depict college life and found many jokes told in very poor taste containing a lot of unnecessary profanity and sexuality. There was also a page on strange stories about sex and drinking at college as well as in everyday life. These stories were meant to entertain readers, but they were unnecessarily vulgar and offensive. Granted, it is humorous to joke about some of the aspects of college other than academic life, but these pages depict college as a place where partying, drinking, and having sex are the essentials.

Although these pages are meant to entertain, they are accessible to young, naive readers—especially to high school students preparing for college. These readers are likely to believe that these pages present a realistic picture of what they can expect on college campuses. Pages such as these should be rated R for young readers.

< @ > :- **"ELECTRONIC BOOK BURNERS"** :-> :-<

By Kyle Belz

Throughout history, the power of print has caused social reform and led to the overthrow of governments. Leaders have realized that to control the flow of ideas in print is to control a nation. The Nazis did this through burning books that went against their beliefs. The Chinese did this by forbidding books or speech that expressed criticism of the government or promote democracy. In the 1950s, even the United States silenced certain ideas by discrediting and blacklisting the individuals that held the "radical" views by labeling them as "Communists." This tendency to silence those with unpopular beliefs extends even into the present. Certain people believe that the World Wide Web contains too many sites on the same subject; therefore, there should be a limit on the number of sites allotted to each topic. Not only is this belief illogical, but this policy, if it were implemented, would violate First Amendment rights.

One reason this policy is unwise is that no two web pages are exactly alike. One need only look at the Green Party of America web site and the Nonviolent web site to realize this. Both of these sites give the individual information on current legislation promoting peace; they also provide access to E-mail to each congressman. However, the Green Party's site also contains information on other issues on the party's platform such as ecological awareness and campaign finance reform. But the nonviolent web site goes more in depth on issues regarding peace, and it also publishes various editorials. Deleting one of these sites creates a void that the other site is not equipped to fill.

The policy of regulating sites is also flawed because the individuals empowered to rank sites could be influenced by their own bias. If this policy were started, the Internet could fall under the control of the rich and powerful. Bribes could become the chief factor in determining which site stays. Imagine the possibilities if this happened. All of the political sites could be reduced to the same basic platform. This would be unhealthy for democracy regardless of which political party seizes control. Although this is only a possibility, it would not be a very shocking development to a nation that already views the government as corrupt.

Thirdly, by following this logic it could be argued that there are too many books with similar plots; therefore, the number should be reduced. Think of the ramifications. One Tom Clancy novel to read! Only one bedtime story to read to your child! These examples may not seem too serious, but it could get worse. Why not allow for only one newspaper since they all report the same news anyway? Now it can be seen that by reducing the number of sites on the web, the population could be subject to propaganda.

Lastly, and most important, such a law would violate the First Amendment. America was founded on the idea that the individual should have the right to voice his or her opinion without fear and to determine the validity of others' opinions. This law would bypass such individual rights and deny the population freedom of consciousness as an outside authority dictates what will and what will not be expressed. This goes against the whole principle of the Internet being the new democratic forum.

It can be seen that there are many disadvantages to a law regulating the number of sites on the WWW. It belittles our freedom and subjects us to the whims of an outside authority. It could bring the nation into greater corruption as the Internet falls prey to the rich. This struggle for freedom of expression is a battle that has raged for centuries; it is just being moved to a new arena. If we wish to maintain the WWW as a place of free expression, we must be willing to defend it.

A P P E N D I X

MLA FORMAT FOR DOCUMENTATION
OF ONLINE SOURCES

Formats for citation of electronic sources are still developing, but in general, you will be safe if you include the following information:[1]

> Author's Last Name, First. "Title of Work." Title of Complete Work. [protocol and address] [path] [date of access, visit, or message].

For example, if you cite a World Wide Web site, the correct format would be:

> O'Mahoney, Benedict. "The Copyright Website." <http://www.benedict.com/> (24 February 1997>.
> No larger work was noted at the Benedict site; therefore, there is no title of complete work in the citation, just the title of work.

Gopher site:

> Alvarez, Juanita. "Devils Among Us." Published in *Mysterious Strangers.* Gopher/University of Nebraska/about devils (29 February 1997).

E-mail citation:

> Texeido, Pablo. "Devilish People." Personal e-mail (29 February 1997).

If the e-mail is *not* personal, include the address of the sender:

> Gilbert, Steve. "WOW! Summary of Postings. AAHESGIT 117/2." gilbert@clark.net (5 May 1997).

FTP site:

> Alvarez, Juanita. "Dante and Devils." ftp.devils.socio.nebedu/papers (25 January 1997).

Online sources of information for MLA and APA format:

---

[1]Format for citations approved by the Alliance for Computers and Writing.

Alliance for Computers and Writing site: http://wilkes1.wilkes.edu/~writing/electronic.html

Janice Walker's site (source of basic format for citations):

http://www.cas.usf.edu/english/walker/mla.html

Other sites:

http:/www.utexas.edu/depts/uwc/.html/citation.html
http://www.lib.lehigh.edu/footnote/chicelec.html

SYNCHRONOUS COMMUNICATION— MUDS, MOOS, AND MUSHES; REAL-TIME CHATS

Using e-mail, you have become familiar with *asynchronous* discussions— exchanges of information, opinion, or sentiments written and read at your convenience. Sometimes these messages are read very soon after they are written, sometimes not.

If you visit MUDs, MOOs, or MUSHes, you will join the expanding world of *synchronous* online communication. You can log on a specific time of day to "meet" with others across the room, or across the world. Or you might drop in on a twenty-four-hour-a-day chat place to see who's there.

People use these online forums to discuss ideas or procedures, to collaborate on presentations or documents, to brainstorm about ways to solve problems, to plan conferences or events, or just to get acquainted with each other in spontaneous, real-time "talk."

When you hook up to a synchronous discussion, you will become a character in an environment, much like virtual reality. If you wish, you can take on an imaginary persona, or you can be yourself. You can make statements, show emotion, indicate actions, and ask questions. You can describe yourself in terms of eye and hair color, age, gender, race, in any way you wish.

WHAT DO YOU DO WHEN YOU GET TO A MOO?

When you get to a MOO, you will probably want to explore to find out how many "rooms" are in the space and to see who's there. Sometimes you are given (online) a brief description of the space. You are told how many rooms there are and where they are in relation to each other. For example, there may be a lobby or commons area, but there may also be meeting rooms. Some rooms may be in use by classes or private groups. Be sure to "knock" (Instructions are given online) before walking in and observe other rules of common courtesy, including avoiding offensive language.

HOW DO YOU GET TO A MUD, MOO, OR MUSH?

You can access a real-time discussion by *telneting* to the proper address at the appointed time of day, or you can use software such as MUDDweller. Ask your instructor or your computer lab director for specific instructions on telneting to MOOs, MUDs, or MUSHes from your location.

To try a sample MOO, at a prompt on your mainframe computer, type *Telnet moo.daedalus.com* 7777. You will connect with the Daedalus MOO, a place where students and teachers across the country, and even across the world can "hang out" to talk about writing. On the first screen, you will see general directions and a description of the layout of the MOO. Use the commands in the list to explore the "rooms" in the MOO.

BASIC COMMANDS FOR MOOS, MUDS, AND MUSHES

@who Tells you who's there and what they have been doing recently.

@go <placename> Takes you where you want to go in the space. The place name can be a word or a number, depending on how the MOO or MUD is set up.

@join <character's name> Allows you to join someone else. This is a good way to get started. It's sort of like joining a friend at a party when you don't know anyone else there.

@whois <character's name> This command will tell you the real name for someone who is using an alias.

@quit Use this command to leave the MOO or MUD.

@linelength, @wrap, @pagelength If the text seems to scroll off of the screen or run beyond the end of the page, use one of these commands to break the text up to fit on your screen. For example, *@wrap* makes the text function like a word processor, wrapping the words at the end of each line so you don't lose any of the text. *@pagelength* stops the scrolling at a specific point, say 22 lines, the average screenful.

" When you want to say something, use quotation marks to open the statement. You don't have to put quotes at the end of the your statement. Just press *Enter* or *Return.*

:<verb + action> When you want to have your character "do" something, type a verb plus a descriptive phrase. For example, you might type *:laughs at Joe's comment.*

help If you want help with commands. If you know the specific command you want help with, type *help <command>.* Otherwise, follow the menus to the commands.

look Lets you "see" the room you're in.

exam <object> Describes a particular object in the room.

page <character's name + message> Lets you send a message to a character in another room.

mu <character's name + message> This commands mutes a message so that only the person intended to hear the message can "hear" it.

OTHER INFORMATION

If you want to take an online minicourse about real-time communication, go to Patrick Crispen's Web site, http://www.nmusd.k12.ca.us/Resources/Roadmap/map26.html. You will find descriptions of all sorts of synchronous groups.

GAMES

MUDs and MOOs originated with games such as Dungeons and Dragons. To find a complete list of multiuser games, go to http://www.mudconnect.com/frameless.html. This site lists the names of the games and gives information about how to link to the game and people to contact. For more information about MOOs and MUDS, go to http://www.fred.net/cindy/frednet.html.

USING PINE E-MAIL

There are many software packages for e-mail, but Pine is a very popular one. If you read the instructions below for Pine, you may be able to figure out how to use your own software, even if it has a different name. The commands for many e-mail programs are quite similar.

To use Pine, you must first access your mainframe computer and sign on with your User ID and your password. If you need help doing that, ask your instructor or a site assistant.

After you have logged on, you can load the Pine software by typing *pine* at the prompt.

To read your messages, type the letter I to open your Inbox. To see a message, use the arrow keys to move the cursor to the message you want to read and press V to view it.

When you finished reading the message, note the menu at the bottom of the screen. Pine (and many other e-mail programs) is extremely user-friendly. The menu always tells you what is possible. For example, press N to go to the next message, or press R to respond to a message. Press F to forward the message to someone else. Press O to see the commands on the other screen. Press Y to print a message. Press M to get to the main menu, where you can press C to compose a message or A to put addresses in your personal e-mail address book.

Press R to respond to someone else's e-mail to you.

When you see the space to respond, write a message, then press Ctrl-X to send it. When Pine asks you if you want to send to all recipients, answer Y if you wish to send mail to a whole group of people, or N if you wish to write a private message.

When you have finished sending your response, press S to save your message in the saved-messages folder. You will be asked to create a folder. Do so by giving it a name. The message will be automatically deleted from your Inbox. To return to the main menu, type M. To see a list of folders, choose L in the main menu.

SENDING E-MAIL

Now try creating a private message.

At the main menu, press C to compose.

At the To: prompt, enter the e-mail address for your recipient. At the Subject line, enter a descriptive word or phrase.

Press Enter and move to the space where you can type the message. Type the text of your message. If you make an error, move the cursor to the right of the charter and press the backspace key to delete.

To send your message, press Ctrl-X.

Type Y to confirm.

Type M to return to the main menu.

TO ADD ADDRESSES TO YOUR ADDRESS BOOK

On the main menu, choose A to access the Address book. Read the menu on the address book screen. Choose A to add a name to your Address book. Answer the prompts. Enter a nickname for the person, an easy one to remember. The program will then show the full name to confirm the connection. Press Enter to accept the entry. The next time you want to send mail to this person, just type his or her nickname in the To: line on the compose screen, and Pine will fill in the e-mail address and user ID.

Is your e-mail program similar to Pine? Make some notes here to record the process you use.

A P P E N D I X

D

HTML COMMANDS

Here is a basic template for all documents:

```
<HTML><HEAD>
<TITLE>
</TITLE>
</HEAD>
<BODY>
<H1> </H1>
</BODY> </HTML>
```

Headings: To reduce the size of headings, increase the number in the tag. For example, <H2> creates a smaller size heading than <H1>.

Paragraphs: Put <p> at the end of each paragraph.

If you forget to include this tag when you want a paragraph break, your whole file will be one long paragraph. You can also use the <p> tag to create extra blank lines in your document.

Line Breaks: Use <br> at the end of short lines, as in an address.

Ordered lists: Use <ol> to create an ordered list, which will number each item. Then tag each item in the list with <li>. At the end of the list, turn off the <ol> tag by typing </ol>.

Unordered lists: Use <ul> to create an unordered list. Items in this list will have bullets, not numbers, in front of them. Use <li> in front of each item. Close the list by typing </ul>.

Bold, italics, underlining, typewriter text: Tag the items you want to set off by inserting the appropriate tag—<b>, <I>, <u>, and <tt>—before and after the items. Turn off the style at the end of the items by using the same tag with a slash (/), in front of it.

Preformatted text: If you want to include text such as a computer program, song lyrics, or a poem, use <pre> to keep the original item's line breaks and spacing. Turn off preformatted text by using </pre>.

Long quotations: Use the <blockquote> tag. Turn it off when the long quote is finished.

Horizontal rules: To separate sections of your HTML page or to divide text from graphics, use a horizontal rule tag: <hr>. This will insert a straight line across the screen the width of the type.

Inserting graphics: This tag <img src="filename.gif"> tells the software to grab the .gif file you have stored in the same directory or folder with your text files and insert the graphic into the text. If the graphic occurs in the middle of text and you want extra space around the image, include paragraph <p> tags before and after the image.

Note: Some browsers don't display graphics. As a courtesy to your readers, you can provide information about the graphic, so that those who can't see it will at least know what the graphic contains. For example, if you include an image of a rabbit in your text, you could say <img src="rabbit.gif" alt="rabbit">. Then, readers who couldn't see the picture of the rabbit would get the word "rabbit" instead.

Hypertext links: To create a link to another document, use the anchor tag. For example, <A HREF="filename.htm"> Your text here</A>. You can link to places within your own document, too, but using a filename from your own directory or folder.

Links to Internet resources: To create a link to other sites on the Web, just substitute the URL for the filename. For example, if you wish to link to Harcourt Brace's site for this textbook, you would type <A HREF="http://www.hbuk.co.uk"> Writing on the Internet</A>.

Linking to a specific section of a different document: If you want your readers to be able to jump to a specific location in a different document, use the anchor tag and include the name of the document plus the specific keyword that you want to link to. For example, <A HREF="rabbit.htm#diet"> would link to a document about rabbits and the specific part of the document that talks about flowers rabbits like to eat (tulips!).

Hypergraphics: To turn your graphic images into hot buttons that link to other documents, simply embed the tag for the image within the tag for the link. For example, if you want to use a picture of a rabbit as a link to the information about rabbits' diets, you could say <A HREF="http://www.rabbits.edu><img src="rabbit.gif">Rabbit Diet</A>.

Postage stamp images: To save time for readers when they view your files, you can include a small version of the graphic on your page. If they wish to see the larger version, they should click on the small (postage stamp) graphic and the large one will load. For example, if I wish to use a small picture of a rabbit to link to a larger one devouring my flowers, I could say <A HREF=largerabbit.gif><img src="smallrabbit.gif"></A>.

Signature: Just before the closing </HTML> tag in your document, include a signature to identify your home page. The signature should include the e-mail address of a contact person (you), the copyright information, and the date when you last made changes to your document. For example, Copyright @ yourname 1999.

Comments, suggestions, or questions may be sent to <A HREF="mailto: your e-mail address">your e-mail address</A>.

Adding a color background: To change the background color of your document, insert the <BODY BGCOLOR="#xxxxxx> command, replacing xxxxxx with the code for a particular color. For example, if you wish to change the background to blue, the command would be <BODY BGCOLOR- "0000FF">. Here are the codes for other common colors:

White	#FFFFFF
Red	#FF0000
Green	#00FF00
Magenta	#FF00FF
Yellow	#FFFF00
Black	#000000

You can find the code for many more colors at http://www.infi.net/ wwwimages/colorindex.html.

You can also control the color of text, unvisited links, visited links, and the currently active link. For more information about changing colors, consult a guide to HTML.

Making tables: To organize information on a Web page, you can create a table using the <TABLE> tag. To create a table, type <TABLE>. Then type <TR> to create a table row. To insert columns or cells in your table, type <TD>yourtext</TD><TD>yourtext</TD>, etc. If you wish to create a new column, type <TR> again, followed by <TD>s for as many cells as you wish.

For more advanced information about HTML, consult online guides. To search for editors that allow you to create pages without using a lot of code, go to http://www.yahoo.com/Computers/World_Wide_Web/HTML_Editors/. To search for converters that take an existing file from a word-processing program and convert it to HTML, go to http://www.yahoo.com/Computers/ World_Wide_Web/HTML_Converters/.

INDEX